Sir Francis Drake

WILLIAM W. LACE

GREAT EXPLORERS

Sir Francis Drake

WILLIAM W. LACE

CHELSEA HOUSE
PUBLISHERS

An imprint of Infobase Publishing

GREAT EXPLORERS: SIR FRANCIS DRAKE

Copyright © 2009 by Infobase Publishing

Chelsea House
An imprint of Infobase Publishing
132 West 31st Street
New York NY 10001

Library of Congress Cataloging-in-Publication Data
Lace, William W.
 Sir Francis Drake / William W. Lace.
    p. cm. — (Great explorers)
 Includes bibliographical references and index.
 ISBN 978-1-60413-417-9 (hardcover)
 1. Drake, Francis, Sir, 1540?-1596—Juvenile literature. 2. Explorers—Great Britain—Biography—Juvenile literature. 3. Admirals—Great Britain—Biography—Juvenile literature. 4. Voyages around the world—Juvenile literature. I. Title. II. Series.
 G420.D7L34 2009
 910.92—dc22
 [B]   2009015017

Series design by Lina Farinella
Cover design by Keith Trego

Printed in the United States of America

Bang EJB 10 9 8 7 6 5 4 3 2 1

This book is printed on acid-free paper.

CONTENTS

Learning His Trade

A LEGEND IS LIKE AN ACORN. IT STARTS SMALL, THEN GROWS—slowly at first, then more rapidly—until it casts a giant shadow over its humble beginning. There was little ordinary, however, about Sir Francis Drake. His legend burst into full flower during his lifetime and has endured ever since.

Drake was truly larger than life. Son of a humble farmer, he came to be hailed as England's greatest hero and feared as Spain's greatest enemy. He hobnobbed with the richest and most powerful people of the day, including Queen Elizabeth I. He acquired great wealth, mostly by taking it forcibly from others.

He was brave to the point of rashness, whether exchanging broadsides with enemy warships or sailing a lone ship into unknown and uncharted waters. He could be gracious and charming to his foes and yet ruthless with those serving under him. He was, at various times, a slave trader, pirate, privateer

English explorer Francis Drake was one of the most famous and accomplished explorers of his time. He gained much fame and fortune during several voyages in which he plundered Spanish ships laden with gold and other treasure. In 1580, Drake returned to Plymouth after completing a voyage around the world.

(a slightly more legitimate kind of pirate), pioneer, preacher, businessman, politician, and admiral.

Humble Beginnings

Nothing in Drake's background pointed to such a stellar career. For at least a century before his birth in about 1540—the exact year is uncertain—his family had leased a farm near the town of Tavistock in the county of Devon in southwestern England. The Drakes were not poor, the farm covering more than 150 acres of fertile land. The family was on good terms with their over-lords, the Russells. Drake was named for Lord John Russell's son, Francis, who was his godfather.

The head of the family at the time of Drake's birth was John Drake, his grandfather. Edmund, father of Francis Drake, was the second of at least three sons living and working with their father. He is thought to have been married to Anna Myl-waye in 1539, with Francis—eldest of 12 children—born about a year later.

Edmund Drake left the area in 1548 for reasons that are unclear. According to the family tradition set down in *Sir Francis Drake Revived*, written by Francis Drake's chaplain and secretary, Philip Nichols, Edmund was a zealous Protestant who was "forced to fly from his house . . . into Kent" by a "state of persecution" on the part of Roman Catholic sympathizers.

Apprentice Sailor

One story was that Edmund squeezed out a living near the English Channel in Kent by reading prayers to sailors in the king's navy. He was so poor that the family lived on the Medway River in an abandoned ship. Contemporary historian William Camden, who knew Francis Drake and may have heard the story directly, writes, as quoted in Ernle Bradford's *The Wind*

Commands Me, that probably sometime in the 1550s, Edmund was forced "by reason of his poverty to put his son [Francis] to the master of a bark [a small ship], with which he used to coast along the shore, and sometimes to carry merchandise into Zeeland [the Netherlands] and France." Thus, as an apprentice, Francis learned both how to sail on the open sea and to pilot a ship into bays and rivers.

Camden writes that the owner of the ship became so fond of the young man that he willed the vessel to Francis, who, after the old man's death, continued to sail up and down the English Channel. He eventually grew weary of the routine life of a coastal sailor, however, and sold his ship. At about age 20, Francis returned to the city of Plymouth in Devon to seek his fortune with the seafaring Hawkins family.

Another Version of the Story

Drake, however, may have given this account to avoid describing what had really happened to his father. In 1548, Devon legal records show Edmund Drake and John Hawkyng [Hawkins] were charged with having stolen a horse. Edmund was also charged with assaulting a man on a highway and stealing his money. He was pardoned later that year but evidently had fled from Devon.

What is more, he might have left his family, or at least his oldest son, behind. Historian Edmund Howes wrote in 1615, as quoted in *Sir Francis Drake* by Harry Kelsey, that Francis was one of "twelve brethren brought up under his kinsman Sir John Hawkins." The Drakes and Hawkinses were related, and it was not unusual for children to be sent to live with more prosperous family members to be raised and educated.

The Hawkins family made its living on the sea, and a good living it was. The head of the family when Drake was a boy was William Hawkins, who had traded goods supplied by his merchant father along the coasts of Africa and Brazil and made the family one of the wealthiest in the county. He had also, under royal license, raided French and Spanish ships when England's relations with these countries were strained.

Also under William Hawkins's roof were his sons John and William. All the boys would have gone to sea and also, given the family's social position, would have had some instruction in proper dress and manners and at least a basic education.

Their primary education, however, would have been a knowledge of currents, tides, and winds and how to rig a ship's sails. They would also learn, over time, how to attack other ships, storm coastal towns, and take by force what did not belong to them. In other words, they learned piracy.

Drake's tale to Camden might have contained some truth. The Hawkins family in the mid-1550s expanded its fleet to the English Channel, and the young Drake—in his late teens—might have sailed a small ship such as the one he claimed was willed to him.

The Slave Trade

Most of the Hawkins activity, however, was to the south and west rather than the east. At about the same time as Drake would have returned to Plymouth (a city on the coast of Devon, England, southwest of London), John Hawkins was commanding trading missions down the western coast of Africa and from there across the Atlantic Ocean to the West Indies. His cargo was human beings.

The slave trade had been active for decades. Spanish colonists in Central America and the West Indies needed more labor to operate their plantations than was available from the native population. Consequently, Africans were rounded up at gunpoint or sometimes sold to Europeans by rival tribes and then crammed into filthy and unsanitary quarters for journeys that could take as long as six months.

John Hawkins was the first Englishman to transport slaves to the Americas, making voyages in 1562 and 1564. This angered both Portugal, which claimed control over the African coast, and Spain, which wanted a monopoly on trade with its colonies.

The colonists, however, needed slaves and did not much care from whom they were purchased. While trade with the English was officially banned, Hawkins got around the prohibition by bribing officials and, occasionally, by force. Sometimes it was almost a game. The officials would deny Hawkins a license, he would come ashore with armed men and fire some shots into the air, whereupon the Spanish would yield. Thus, the colonists got their slaves and the officials could claim they were overpowered.

It is not known if Drake was on either voyage, but he was definitely part of the next one, although it was not led by Hawkins. Spain and Portugal had protested so vigorously against him that Queen Elizabeth issued a public order forbidding him to leave England, though some of her chief officials—and perhaps she, herself—had secretly financed him and shared in the profits.

Lovell's Voyage

Although Hawkins put together the next voyage, he gave command to a cousin, John Lovell. The expedition set sail from Plymouth on November 9, 1566. There were three ships: the *Paul*, on which Lovell sailed, the smaller *Solomon*; and the still-smaller *Pasco*. Which ship carried Drake is not known, but given his connection to the Hawkins family, he was probably a junior officer.

The squadron first stopped, as usual, at Tenerife in the Canary Islands to take on supplies. From there, it went south to Cape Verde, the westernmost point of Africa, where Lovell seized a Portuguese ship and its cargo, which included slaves.

He then raided two more Portuguese islands, capturing four more ships. There is no record of another attack, so enough slaves might have been captured to proceed across the Atlantic.

After a short stop at the island of Margarita off the coast of present-day Venezuela to take on fresh supplies, the ships sailed to the town of Borburata on the mainland. Here, Lovell joined forces with Jean Bontemps, a French pirate, and, after a brief show of force, was able to sell some of the slaves.

Lovell was not as fortunate at the next stop—Rio de la Hacha, to the west around the northern coast of South America. The governor, Miguel de Castellanos, had been humiliated by Hawkins years before and was determined not to yield to the English again. He refused to give Lovell a license to trade.

English Defeat

This must have been a humiliating experience for the English. Many years later, in *Sir Francis Drake Revived*, Nichols wrote that Drake still was angered by "the wrongs received at Rio de la Hacha."

Lovell decided to return to England. When the squadron landed in Plymouth in September 1567, Drake learned that his father had died the preceding December. There was little time for mourning, however, as Hawkins was already mounting another expedition. Queen Elizabeth had not only withdrawn his confinement to England, but also had contributed two of her own ships, the *Jesus of Lubeck,* which she had also loaned to Hawkins for his second voyage, and the *Minion*.

Four of Hawkins's ships rounded out the fleet, including the small *Judith*. One account of the voyage asserts that Drake was in command of the *Judith* from the start. Another, however, places him as an officer on the *Jesus of Lubeck*.

The "Troublesome Voyage"

Hawkins's own account written two years later was titled *The Third Troublesome Voyage*, and it was so from the very first. Only four days after sailing on October 2, 1567, the fleet encountered a storm so fierce that Hawkins considered abandoning

John Hawkins (*center, with slaves and inset*) was the first established English slave trader. The slave trade was very profitable and Queen Elizabeth I supported him by donating two of her own ships, the *Jesus of Lubeck* and the *Minion*. At about 23 years old, Drake took his first journey to the New World, with Hawkins on one of his fleet of ships.

the entire venture. Eventually, the ships, which had lost contact with one another, managed to regroup in the Canary Islands, where repairs were made.

The ships reached the African coast at Cabo Blanco about two weeks later. There, they found three Portuguese ships and Hawkins appropriated one of them—a small ship called a caravel. According to a report written many years later, Hawkins put Drake in command of the captured ship—the *Gratia Dei*, or "Grace of God." If so, it would have been his first independent command since it is unlikely he would have been transferred from the *Judith* to a much smaller vessel.

Hawkins would add two more ships to his fleet before leading an attack on a native village a few miles inland of Cape Verde. The attack was a failure. About 25 men, including Hawkins, were wounded by poisoned arrows, and a few later died. Only nine slaves were captured and additional raids through November and December resulted in a total of about 150 captives—not enough to make a profitable trip to the Americas.

In January, however, Hawkins enlisted the help of two native chiefs to mount an assault on a rival tribe on the island of Conga in the Tagarin River in present-day Sierra Leone. About 850 captives were taken, but Hawkins's native allies, who had promised to turn over all prisoners, vanished in the middle of the night, taking about 650 with them. However, as Hawkins wrote in *The Third Troublesome Voyage*, "we had obtained between four hundred and five hundred negroes, wherewith we thought it somewhat reasonable to seek the coast of the West Indies . . . to countervail [offset] our charges with some gains."

In the Caribbean

After a passage across the Atlantic of about seven weeks, the fleet made landfall at Dominica in the Antilles Islands, West Indies, proceeding on to Margarita and then to the mainland port of Borburata. Here Hawkins discovered that his usual methods—a request followed by a refusal followed by a show of force—no longer worked. The town was too strong to be stormed and, after a few fruitless weeks, the fleet set sail for its second target—Rio de la Hacha.

A few days earlier, Hawkins had dispatched two ships to scout the port at Rio de la Hacha. One was the *Angel* and the other was the *Judith*, which at this point was, indeed, commanded by Drake. As they approached, the Spaniards, who had received a warning from Borburata, opened fire from recently installed gun placements. The English returned fire, one cannonball going through the governor's house.

The *Judith* and *Angel* withdrew out of range, blockading the port and waiting on the rest of the fleet, which appeared on June 10. Hawkins sent a message to the governor, Castellanos, who refused his request to trade just as he had refused Lovell's. Rio de la Hacha, however, was not as well fortified as Borburata, and Hawkins had a far stronger force than Lovell had when he tried and was refused a trading license. He stormed ashore with 200 men and captured the town, seizing the treasury and taking several hostages.

Castellanos now had no choice but to make a deal. Hawkins agreed to return the treasury, except for 4,000 pesos in gold as a ransom for the hostages. In addition, he was allowed to sell about 200 slaves.

At the next stop, the small town of Santa Marta on the coast of present-day Venezuela, a show of force was all that was necessary before the Spaniards relented and allowed the purchase of about 110 slaves.

Only 57 captives now remained aboard the ships, many having died during the voyage. With hurricane season approaching, Hawkins decided to head for home. He had amassed the equivalent of about $4 million, enough to pay off the queen and others who had financed the venture, with plenty left to turn a handsome profit.

Blown Off Course

The fleet sailed north, intending to go around Cuba and then south of Florida into the Atlantic. On August 12, 1568, however, at the western tip of Cuba, a hurricane hit, driving the ships into the Gulf of Mexico, where none of the sailors had ever been. The damage was great; the planks along the bottom of the *Jesus of Lubeck* had separated so much that fish were swimming in the hold. The nearest harbor, a passing Spanish ship told Hawkins, was San Juan d'Ulua, a small island town on the eastern coast of Mexico that served as a port for the city of Vera Cruz.

The Spanish ship also told Hawkins that the annual supply fleet from Spain was due in San Juan d'Ulua at any time. The English commander had no wish to encounter the heavily armed Spanish warships he knew would be escorting the fleet, since he had been where he was not supposed to be and doing what he was not supposed to do. However, he had no choice.

When the English ships arrived on September 15, the Spanish colonists thought they were the supply fleet and sent officials out in a small boat to welcome it. Instead, Hawkins captured the officials and then the town. He reassured the citizens that they would come to no harm and that he would pay them for any supplies taken.

On September 17, the Spanish fleet appeared. Hawkins had enough ships to blockade it from the harbor and thus be safe from attack, but hesitated. Another storm was brewing, and he was afraid that if the Spanish fleet was denied a safe harbor and severely damaged, it might provoke a Spanish backlash against England. He negotiated with Don Martin Enriquez, the Spanish viceroy who had accompanied the fleet, and the two sides reached an uneasy truce. Hostages were exchanged to guard against treachery, and the Spanish ships were admitted to the harbor where the two fleets anchored at point-blank range from one another.

Surprise Attack

At first, all was cordial. Don Enriquez, however, felt humiliated at having had to negotiate with men he considered pirates. He secretly sent word to Vera Cruz, and 120 heavily armed soldiers were slipped aboard the Spanish ships. The surprise attack was planned for the morning of September 23, 1568.

The English, however, were not taken completely by surprise. Hawkins had suspected treachery, and when the signal

DRAKE'S "FORSAKING" OF HAWKINS

When John Hawkins wrote in his account of the *Third Troublesome Voyage* that, on the morning after the battle at San Juan d'Ulau, he discovered that the ship *Judith*, commanded by Francis Drake, "forsook us in our misery," he cast a pall over Drake's career that has lingered throughout the centuries. Although he is not known to have leveled such charges at the time both had returned to England, the implication was that Drake had deserted his commanding officer, perhaps to keep as much of the Spanish treasure as possible.

Two other eyewitness accounts, however, are less accusatory. One, in fact, by Jeb Hortop, says that Hawkins "willed Master Francis Drake to come in with the *Judith*, and to lay the *Minion* aboard, to take in men and other things needful, and to go out, and so he did." The other, by Miles Philips of the *Minion*, says only that "The same night the said bark the Judith lost us, we being in great necessity."

Drake is not known to have suffered any consequences for his actions, although unsubstantiated Spanish sources said he was imprisoned. The quotations of Hortop and Philips are found in *Francis Drake: Privateer* edited by John Hampden.

for the attack was given—too early, as it turned out—the English quickly sprang to arms.

Guns from both fleets erupted against one another. The *Angel* was sunk and three more English ships totally disabled. Only Drake's *Judith*, which had been at the end of the English line, managed to avoid being damaged.

The Spaniards then sent a fireship—an unmanned vessel loaded with combustible material and set ablaze—toward the damaged *Jesus of Lubeck*. Hawkins saw that his position was hopeless. He began to abandon the *Jesus*, taking what men and treasure he could into the *Minion,* and signaled Drake to approach with the *Judith* and help, which he did.

The only English ships able to sail—the *Minion* and the *Judith*—were able to clear the harbor, but the Spaniards were in no condition to pursue them. Behind, on the *Jesus* or swimming for shore, were the rest of Hawkins's sailors and the surviving slaves.

As night fell, an uneasy quiet fell over San Juan d'Ulau. At dawn the next morning, Hawkins found himself alone. Drake and the *Judith* had vanished, leaving him with the severely overcrowded *Minion*. Hawkins clearly thought he had been deserted, writing later in *The Third Troublesome Journey* (without using Drake's name) that the *Judith* "forsook us in our great misery."

Lingering Questions

Historians and biographers have speculated ever since on Drake's actions. Some have claimed that the wind increased and Drake lost contact with the *Minion* and thought it had been wrecked. Others have said that the *Judith* itself was in bad shape and could not take the time to look for Hawkins. The other possibility—one that would haunt Drake for the rest of his career—was that he took advantage of darkness to abandon his commander and slip away with what portion of the treasure he had taken from the *Jesus*.

Drake reached Plymouth on January 20, 1569. Hawkins made it to England only a few days later, but after a much more difficult journey. His men were starving, having survived by eating rats and mice, and dozens of the crew had died along the way. The English sailors that were abandoned in San Juan d'Ulua were even more unfortunate. More than 200 were executed by the Spaniards, died in captivity, or escaped into the jungle only to be killed by natives.

How Drake explained himself to Hawkins, and what Hawkins's reaction was, are not known. The two men would serve together again, but not in the same way. Hawkins's days of raiding Spanish possessions in the New World were over, but not Drake's. Perhaps because of a desire for revenge and perhaps because of a sense of personal guilt for his desertion of Hawkins, he became a bitter and unyielding enemy of Spain.

Drake was now about 29 years old. He had learned seamanship and piracy and was ready to employ both against Spain. It would not be too long before he was able to do so.

2

"El Draque"

IN 1568 AN ENGLISH SAILOR HELD PRISONER BY THE SPANIARDS named the captains who had served under Hawkins on his ill-fated expedition. His list did not include Francis Drake. Such obscurity would not last long. Between 1570 and 1573, Drake made three raids on the West Indies and Central America. Afterward, his name was on everyone's lips— praised in England, cursed in Spain.

In 1570 relations between Spain and England were at a low ebb. Spanish troops occupied the Netherlands, repressing the largely Protestant population with whom the English sympathized. Then, when Spanish ships carrying money to the Netherlands to pay troops were forced by a storm to take refuge in Plymouth, Queen Elizabeth appropriated the treasure. Spain responded by seizing all English shipping and goods in Dutch harbors.

Both England and France—also a rival of Spain—commissioned privateers to harass Spanish shipping along the English

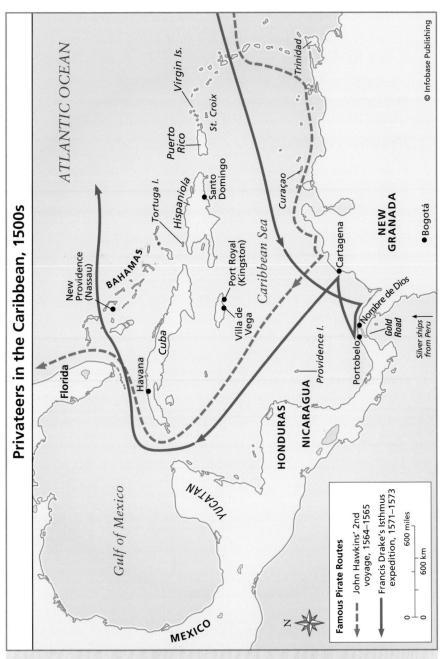

Privateers in the Caribbean, 1500s

ATLANTIC OCEAN

Virgin Is.

St. Croix

Puerto Rico

Santo Domingo

Hispaniola

Tortuga I.

New Providence (Nassau)

BAHAMAS

Port Royal (Kingston)

Villa de Vega

Cuba

Havana

Florida

Gulf of Mexico

MEXICO

YUCATAN

HONDURAS

NICARAGUA

Providence I.

Caribbean Sea

Curaçao

Trinidad

Cartagena

NEW GRANADA

Bogotá

Nombre de Dios

Portobelo

Gold Road

Silver ships from Peru

Famous Pirate Routes

John Hawkins' 2nd voyage, 1564–1565

Francis Drake's Isthmus expedition, 1571–1573

0   600 miles

0   600 km

N

© Infobase Publishing

Privateers—private warships supported by a national government—were com-missioned to attack enemy vessels and capture any treasure that was on board. Although they did not take orders from naval commanders, these raiders engaged in warfare and were a large part of the military force. Queen Elizabeth I hired some of her best sailors to work as privateers, including Hawkins and Drake.

Channel and in the North Sea, but Drake had seen the riches of Spain's New World possessions and how lightly they were defended. He determined to take advantage of both, thus enriching himself and taking personal revenge for what he—and all of England—considered Spanish treachery at San Juan de U'lau.

Prison or Profit?

Most of Drake's actions after the Hawkins expedition are unknown. One unverified Spanish account says that he had escaped on the *Judith* with most of the treasure and, when his desertion of Hawkins was revealed, was imprisoned by Queen Elizabeth. Another story claimed that Drake and Hawkins split the loot between themselves and told everyone else it had been lost.

Whatever its source, Drake had enough money to buy a substantial house in Plymouth, call himself a merchant, and get married. Very little is known about his wife, Mary Newman. They had no children and Mary spent most of their 12 years of marriage alone on shore.

He also had enough funds to mount an expedition, although he may have had additional backers, possibly even the Hawkins brothers. In 1570, less than six months after his wedding, Drake sailed from Plymouth in command of two small ships—the *Swan* and the *Dragon*. It was a tiny force, but Drake had no need of a larger one, at least at the moment. According to *Sir Francis Drake Revived*, his mission was "to gain such intelligence as might further him to get some amend." In other words, it was a scouting mission.

Drake accomplished his purpose so well that almost no record of the voyage exists. He was after information, not plunder, and what he found would turn out to be valuable, indeed. Since the Hawkins raid, Spain had increased its defenses in the Caribbean, fortifying coastal towns and positioning a squadron of warships under the command of Diego Flores de Valdez. Still, however, it was a force insufficient to protect such a vast area.

The Gold Road

One of the most vulnerable, and yet most valuable, links in Spain's treasure chain were the few miles of land—about 50 (80 kilometers)—across the Isthmus of Panama that separate the Caribbean from the Pacific Ocean. Much of Spain's wealth came from gold and silver mined in Chile and Peru. Such cargo was far too valuable to risk in the long, dangerous voyage through the Strait of Magellan at the tip of South America. Instead, it was shipped to the city of Panama, then taken by mule trains through mountain passes and jungle trails to the headwaters of the Chagres River. From there, the treasure continued—on rafts in the rainy season and on mules in the dry season—to the port town of Nombre de Dios on the Caribbean side. There, it was stored until it could be loaded into ships bound for Spain.

This narrow highway of silver and gold was Drake's target. But first, he returned to England, enlisting more men and gaining more investors, tempting them with descriptions of the riches he would bring back. He sailed again early in 1571, this time taking only the light, swift *Swan* and a crew of about 30 men.

He reached Panama in February only to learn that a French privateer, Nicholas des Isles, had preceded him. Des Isles had brought with him Pedro Mandinga, a *cimarrone*, or escaped African slave, who led the French up the Chagres River in a small boat to the town of Venta Cruces. Before they could attack the town, however, Mandinga deserted. With their guide gone, the French retreated downstream only to find that de Valdez had been alerted to their presence. They escaped, but the Spaniards had been warned about attacks on the isthmus.

The First Attack

Drake made no secret of his presence. On February 21, a Spanish cargo ship bound for Nombre de Dios and anchored offshore was approached by a pinnace, a small boat propelled by either oars or sails. Two small cannons known as culverins were mounted on the bow, and the English crew was heavily armed with swords, bows and arrows, and firearms known as arquebuses.

When Drake's men tried to board the vessel, the Spaniards resisted, but they were poorly armed. The English opened fire, killing four of the defenders and wounding two of the dignitaries aboard. The Spaniards cut their anchor rope, allowing the ship to drift ashore and the passengers and crew to escape into the jungle.

Meanwhile, a second Spanish merchant ship had appeared. It was promptly chased ashore by the English, its crew escaping. Drake and his men spent a day looting their prizes and, when they were finished, left behind a bold and impudent note to the former owners. Possibly written by Drake himself, it claimed the English had only wanted to talk and had attacked only after the Spaniards had refused. Furthermore, the note said, the English had no fear of de Valdez's ships sent to find them and threatened that, if attacked, they would fight back.

Only a few days later, Drake succeeded where des Isles had failed, going up the Chagres River to Venta Cruces. He found no gold or silver, but did seize merchandise, mostly rich cloth, valued by the Spaniards at 100,000 pesos. He carried the loot back downriver to be loaded onto the *Swan*, which then escaped to the nearby Bastimentos Islands as de Valdez searched in vain.

Over the next few weeks, the *Swan* struck repeatedly, intercepting and looting about a dozen cargo vessels. There was so much taken—the Spaniards later valued it at 230,000 pesos—that Drake kept two of the better ships so that he could store it all.

In May 1571, Drake conducted another raid up the Chagres River, seizing four boats and their cargos before returning to the *Swan*. It was a rich haul, the Spaniards later complaining,

Caca Fogo.

Caca Plata.

In the late sixteenth century, England and Spain were fierce rivals. Attacking and plundering Spanish treasure ships sailing from what is now Mexico and South America brought riches to the coffers of England, the queen, and to Drake. Drake was a huge threat to Spanish vessels, and he was greatly feared. The Spanish called Drake "El Draque," or the Dragon.

as quoted by Sugden, that the English had taken "merchandise of 40,000 ducats, velvets and taffetas, besides other merchandise, with gold and silver."

"El Draque"

Spain now knew with whom it was dealing. A letter to King Philip of Spain in May 1571 named Drake and said, as quoted by Sugden, that he was "so fully in possession of [the coast] . . . that traffic dare not sail." Another letter quoted by Sugden, this one from an official at Nombre de Dios, complained that the town had spent 4,000 pesos "in search of this corsair . . . and he has always had the luck to escape." In time, the Spaniards would twist the name Drake into "El Draque," or "The Dragon."

Drake now decided it was time to return to England. Before sailing, however, he found a place in which to hide during future voyages. It was a natural harbor, screened from view by the jungle and with plenty of fresh water and wild game nearby. The fowl, in fact, were so plentiful that he named the site Port Pheasant.

A few weeks later, Drake was back at Plymouth. He had left with one ship, but returned with three—all packed with costly goods and some gold and silver. The total value was about 66,000 British pounds, double what Hawkins had taken in on all three of his slaving expeditions. His backers were delighted, but Drake—although considerably enriched—was eager to strike at Spain again, this time against the overland treasure route.

Next Voyage

By May of 1572, the next voyage was ready. The Hawkins brothers were definitely among the backers since it was one of their ships, the *Pasco*, that accompanied the *Swan*. Also present were three pinnaces—*Bear*, yet another *Minion*, and *Lion*—that had been disassembled and stowed away. Drake commanded the *Pasco*, and his younger brother John was the leader of the

Swan. Also part of the company was another brother, Joseph. They took 73 crewmen, all but one under the age of 30, supplies for a year and all manner of weaponry.

The ships left Plymouth on May 24. Twenty-eight days later they reached Port Pheasant only to find a note left for Drake the year before by another English captain warning him that the Spaniards had discovered the site. Since the harbor entrance was narrow enough to be defended, he decided to stay there anyway, building a heavily fortified stockade.

As the men were working, a ship approached the harbor, but it was English, captained by James Raunce. Raunce had served with Drake under John Hawkins. Raunce agreed to help in the upcoming attack on Nombre de Dios, and the company now numbered about 100 men.

Drake decided to attack at the first opportunity. In late July he sailed to the Isle of Pines, where he left Raunce and the larger ships. Taking the pinnaces and 53 men, he rowed quietly through the night to Nombre de Dios, taking up station outside the town to wait for dawn. His men, however, grew nervous. The town was larger than many had expected, and some began to lose their nerve.

Taking the Town

Drake sensed the loss of morale and decided to launch the raid at once. He divided his forces, leading half up the main street toward the marketplace while the rest, under John Drake and John Oxenham, approached from one side. The Spaniards, however, had been alerted, and the mayor had collected a few armed men at one end of the marketplace. As Drake and his men charged them—trumpet blaring and drums beating—they fired a few shots. Most went wild, but one struck Drake in the leg. At about the same time, John Drake and Oxenham rushed in from the side. The Spaniards broke ranks and ran, and the English held the town.

They moved quickly to the mayor's house where, according to *Sir Francis Drake Revived*, they found "a pile of bars of silver . . . seventy foot in length . . . each bar between thirty-five and forty pounds in weight." Drake, however, was after bigger game. He ordered his men to leave the silver alone, then led them to the storeroom on the waterfront where much more treasure was awaiting transport to Spain.

Ordering his brother John and Oxenham to break down the door, Drake led a small group into the street from where they could fire at any foes. Just as the assault on the door was about to begin, Drake fell down in a faint. Only then did his men notice his wounded leg and how much it had bled. They quickly abandoned the storeroom, tied a scarf around Drake's leg, and retreated to the pinnaces. They reasoned that if they saved his life, he would lead them to other treasures whereas if he died, they would be lost.

Once recovered, Drake knew that Nombre de Dios would be reinforced perhaps beyond his ability to take it again. Raunce was discouraged and took his men back to England, but Drake simply turned to another target—Cartagena, the largest city on the northern coast of South America and the hub of Spanish shipping. News of his attack at Nombre de Dios had spread, however, and while he was able to take three ships, he was unable to do much more.

Another Plan

Drake considered his options. The treasure being carried to Nombre de Dios remained his target, but he now decided that, if he could not capture it in the town, he would do so before it could reach the town. One factor in his thinking might have been the presence of Diego, a cimarrone who had attached himself to the English in the raid on Nombre de Dios and who had won Drake's confidence and friendship. Not only was Diego able to provide more knowledge of the treasure route, he also offered to enlist the help of some of his comrades.

Meanwhile, Drake concluded that he had too few men for the three pinnaces and the two larger ships. He sacrificed the *Swan*, but did not want to anger John Drake by depriving him of his command. He secretly ordered a carpenter to bore holes in the ship's hull and then, when the ship sank, he commiserated with his brother over what he said was an unexplainable accident.

John Drake was soon to have another assignment—negotiating with bands of cimarrones. Eventually, cimarrone leaders were brought aboard the *Pasco* and an agreement reached whereby, according to *Sir Francis Drake Revived*, "they should have some opportunity to wreak wrongs on the Spaniards [and] we hoping that now our voyage would be bettered." This alliance, when they learned of it, frightened the Spaniards. One report, quoted in Sudgen's book, told King Philip that it was "most lamentable" that the groups had joined forces "for the blacks are numerous."

Together, the English and cimarrones began building a fort on an island that Drake intended to use as a base from which to attack the isthmus. He was so pleased with his new allies that he named it Fort Diego.

Death and Disease

The first days of 1573, however, brought the expedition to its lowest point. Francis Drake had been away from the island for months, harassing ships near Cartagena. He returned in early January to find that his brother John had been killed in a botched attack on a Spanish ship.

Then, with morale already low, an epidemic, now thought to have been yellow fever, swept over the company. Twenty-eight men died, including Drake's other brother, Joseph. The spirit of the survivors was so low that they named their hideaway Slaughter Island. Even though he now had only about 35 men left, Drake was determined to make another attempt at the treasure route. Finally, in February, the cimarrones brought the news that the treasure would shortly be on its way overland.

Drake sprang into action. He took 18 of his men plus 30 cimarrones and marched inland. His intent was to ambush

VISION OF THE PACIFIC

One of the most dramatic events in the life of Francis Drake occurred during his 1572–1573 raid on Panama. He was told by a cimmarone, a slave escaped from the Spaniards, that there was a tall tree about halfway across the Isthmus of Panama from which the Pacific Ocean might be seen. The event was recorded by Philip Nichols, later Drake's chaplain and secretary, in *Sir Francis Drake Revived*:

> After our Captain [Drake] has ascended to this bower with the chief Cimaroon, and having as it pleased God at that time, by reason of the breeze, a very fair day, had seen that sea of which he had heard such golden reports, he besought Almighty God of His goodness to give him lift and leave to sail once in an English ship in that sea. And then, calling up all the rest of our men, he acquainted John Oxenham especially with this his petition and purpose, if it would please god to grant him that happiness; who, understanding it presently protested that unless our Captain did beat him from his company he would follow him, by God's grace.

As it happened, Oxenham was to sail in the Pacific even before Drake. He crossed the isthmus in 1576 and built a small ship with which to raid Spanish ships, but was caught, imprisoned, and eventually executed.

the mule train before it could get to Venta Cruces. On the way, an event occurred that was to change his life. The cimarrones led him to a tall tree near the top of which was an observation platform. From this height, looking west, he could see the broad expanse of the Pacific Ocean, a sight no Englishman had ever beheld. Falling on his knees, he prayed that he might, at some time or other, sail there.

Meanwhile, however, there was treasure to capture. Told by a cimarrone scout that a mule train was on its way from Panama, the English stationed themselves in the darkness outside the town. Before the mule train arrived from the west, however, a lone rider came up the road the other way from Venta Cruces. One of Drake's men, Robert Pike, jumped up, his white shirt glowing in the moonlight. The rider saw him and raced on down the road. The rider warned the mule train and another opportunity had been missed.

Teaming with Le Testu

Drake, however, was determined to try again and was convinced that the overland route was the best point of attack. He solved one of his concerns, a lack of men, by teaming up with French privateer Guillaume Le Testu and his 70-man crew. They planned, instead of intercepting the mule train before it reached Venta Cruces, to take the bolder step of seizing it just before it reached the coast at Nombre de Dios. This would also make it easier to escape afterward.

The two commanders sailed in pinnaces up the Rio Francisco a few miles east of the town and then set off overland with 25 French and English sailors and their cimarrone allies.

The group took up position just west of the town. Then, at dawn on April 1, they heard the sound of bells on the bridles of almost 200 mules. This time there would be no mistakes. As the attackers swept down on them, the Spanish soldiers fired a few shots and then ran into the jungle. One of the shots, however, hit Le Testu in the stomach.

The haul was tremendous, some 30 tons of gold and silver, far more than the raiders could take away. When each man had as much as he could carry, the rest was hastily buried. The group then headed for the Rio Francisco, leaving Le Testu behind, at his request, with two comrades.

Emergency Trip

When they reached the rendezvous site, the pinnaces were nowhere in sight. Drake's followers thought they had been captured, but he insisted they had only been delayed by an overnight storm and set out to find them. He and three volunteers went downriver to the coast, built a raft out of logs and fallen tree limbs, and fashioned a sail out of burlap sacks. It took them six hours to work their way around a spit of land to a point where they could, indeed, see the pinnaces approaching.

The sailors aboard the pinnaces, seeing their captain and only three companions all ragged and sunburned, thought the mission had failed. Eagerly, they questioned him, and Drake, with dramatic flair, pulled a large circlet of gold from his jacket and said, according to *Sir Francis Drake Revived*, that "our voyage was made."

Drake had not forgotten Le Testu. When the rest of his men and the treasure they carried were brought safely aboard the *Pasco*, he led a small party back to the Rio Francisco. The French captain, however, was gone, and the Spaniards had found and recovered most of the buried silver.

All that remained was to give the Frenchmen their share of the treasure, reward the cimarrones with gifts of cloth and tools, and head for home. The *Pasco* was thought to be too small and old for the return voyage, so Drake took a Spanish frigate he had captured, snapped up second prize near Cartagena, and set sail for England.

On August 9, 1573, two strange ships were seen in Plymouth harbor, from which the *Swan* and *Pasco* had sailed more than a year before. It was a Sunday morning, and most of the townspeople were in church. When the rumor began to spread that Drake had returned, the congregations melted away to the point, according to *Sir Francis Drake Revived,* that "very few or none remained with the preacher."

Around the World—Atlantic

DRAKE'S THREE RAIDS ON THE NEW WORLD HAD LIFTED HIM from obscurity to national prominence. He was now one of the wealthiest men in England, his share of the third voyage having been at least £20,000 (pounds). But bold and profitable as the raids were, they only set the stage for what was to come—an epic and unprecedented voyage around the world.

When Drake arrived in Plymouth in 1573, however, that journey was years in the future. Politically speaking, he had come home at an awkward time. While he had been away, relations between England and Spain had improved, and Queen Elizabeth found it embarrassing to have the nation talking about Drake's exploits.

As a result, he was asked to drop out of sight. Nothing is known about him until two years later in Ireland, when he commanded three ships in the service of the earl of Essex, who was trying to put down a revolt there. There was little noteworthy about the Irish interlude except that it was then that he became

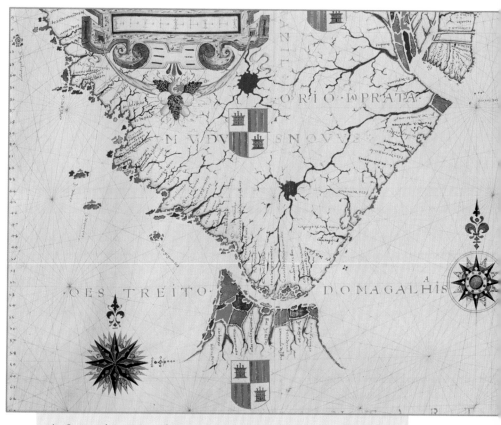

In September 1578, after a voyage through the Strait of Magellan (*above, at bottom between the land masses*), Drake lost his smallest ship, the *Marigold*, and all men onboard to the sea. The ship Drake commanded, the *Golden Hind*, was then separated from the *Elizabeth* and blown far south. Drake became the first Englishman to navigate the strait and to discover that there was open water below the South American continent, which was not known at the time. This map of South America and the Strait of Magellan was published in 1571.

friends with Thomas Doughty, one of Essex's aides, who would play a prominent role in his voyage to the Pacific Ocean.

It had been only 65 years since Antoine de Abreu of Portugal had become the first European to see the Pacific, sailing there from the Indian Ocean in 1511. Two years later, Vasco Nuñez de Balboa saw the Pacific from Panama, and in 1519

Ferdinand Magellan became the first to sail from the Atlantic to the Pacific through the strait that bears his name, although he did not live to complete the voyage around the world.

Dangerous Passage

Strong and variable winds, tricky currents, submerged rocks and the very narrowness of the passage made the Strait of Magellan extremely treacherous. It was used only because navigators did not realize that there was open water below South America. They thought instead that Tierra del Fuego, the large island south of the strait, was a vast, unexplored continent named Terra Australis. By Drake's time, Spain had almost abandoned use of the strait, preferring to build its ships on the Pacific side and send goods overland between the oceans.

Drake was not the first Englishman to command a ship in the Pacific. Relations with Spain had again taken a turn for the worse in 1576. Drake's former lieutenant, John Oxenham, succeeded in crossing the Isthmus of Panama and building a small ship on the western shore. He seized some unprotected Spanish ships but was captured and eventually executed.

At the same time Oxenham was languishing in prison, Drake was putting forth his proposal. Such a scheme would require powerful supporters, and Drake had them. He had obtained from the earl of Essex a letter of introduction to Sir Francis Walsingham, one of Queen Elizabeth's chief officers. His other backers included Christopher Hatton and the earl of Leicester, two of the queen's favorites. These men, and others, were those who saw all-out war with Spain as inevitable and wanted to do everything possible to harass the enemy beforehand and to make a profit for themselves in the bargain.

Secrecy Above All

Everything, however, had to be done with the strictest secrecy, and even today exactly what Drake's original plan was, and how it may have changed, is uncertain. Even in his first private meeting with Walsingham, he refused to put anything in writing. According to a manuscript by John Cooke, who took part in the voyage and got his information directly from Drake, he feared that Elizabeth might be succeeded by another ruler more friendly to Spain and then "will mine own hand be a witness against myself." It was a legitimate concern. Elizabeth was unmarried and childless, the succession was uncertain, and only 18 years earlier England had been ruled by Mary Tudor, who had been married to Philip of Spain.

Eventually, Walsingham would present a written document to the queen. This document, of which only fragments have survived, mentions people "not under the obedience of princes, so there is great hope of . . . spices, drugs . . . special commodities." The voyage was to last 13 months, of which 5 were to be spent sailing along the coast to get knowledge of the "princes and countries there."

On the face of it, the mission seems to have been intended for trade, and some historians have interpreted it as such. Others think Drake's orders were specifically to plunder Spanish shipping up to 30 degrees south, the latitude just north of the port of Valparaiso in Chile.

It is possible that Drake's instructions combined both trade and disruption of Spanish shipping. Queen Elizabeth was known for issuing secret orders so that, if a privateer such as Drake were captured, she could deny all knowledge of his actions. She even once said about Drake, as quoted by Sugden, "If need be the gentleman careth not if I should disavow him."

Meeting with the Queen

John Cooke, who was on the voyage and who had his information directly from Drake, wrote of a meeting sometime in 1577 between Drake and the queen arranged by Walsingham. "Drake," Elizabeth said, as quoted in Hampden's book, "so it is

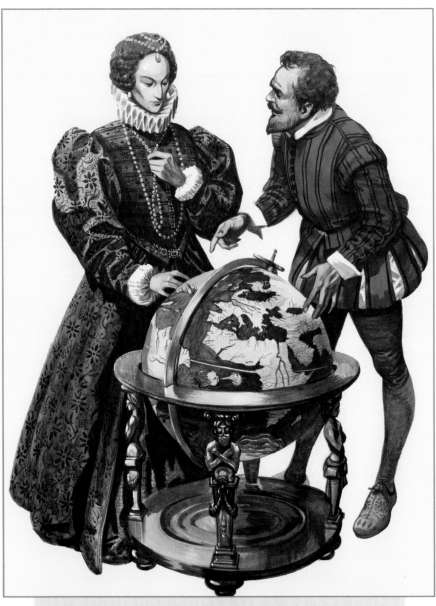

Although Queen Elizabeth I (*left*) opposed Drake (*right*) in public, privately she enjoyed the great riches she received from his bloody expeditions against the Spanish. She ordered that all written accounts of his voyages and her involvement in them be kept secret, and any participants were threatened with death should they reveal any information.

that I would gladly be revenged on the King of Spain, for divers injuries that I have received." She added that she thought Drake was the only man who could obtain such revenge for her. When Drake outlined his plan, the queen agreed and added that if any word of the true nature of the voyage leaked out, those responsible "should lose their heads." She particularly wanted to keep the plot secret from her chief minister, Lord Burghley, who opposed friction with Spain.

With his own money and what he could raise from his backers—including a hefty sum from the queen—Drake began to put his fleet together. He had the *Pelican* as his flagship along with the *Elizabeth*, the *Marigold*, another *Swan*, and the *Benedict*. There were also four pinnaces stowed away, ready to be assembled later.

Rounding out the company were about 160 men and boys. The faithful Diego was there, as were another Drake brother, Thomas, and a cousin, John. In addition to ordinary sailors, there were carpenters, a blacksmith, a botanist, and several musicians to entertain the admiral. Also aboard was a chaplain, Francis Fletcher, whose narrative would be the basis for *The World Encompassed*, an account of the voyage.

In addition to the crew, there were about a dozen "gentlemen" who had signed on in search of adventure. Thomas Doughty, now an attorney, was among them. The gentlemen would soon arouse the anger of the ordinary sailors by lounging about and refusing to do any manual work.

False Information

The public and all of the ships' crewmen except for Drake's most trusted officers were told that the expedition was bound for the Mediterranean on a trading mission. The story might have fooled the sailors, but not the Spaniards, who had spies everywhere. They knew who his backers were—even the queen—but they did not know where he planned to strike. The Spanish ambassador, Antonio de Guaras, wrote to King Philip, as quoted in Harry Kelsey's *Sir Francis Drake*, that Spain must "know the location in order to send them to the bottom of the sea."

Even before the start of the voyage at least one member of the party began to question Drake's authority. Thomas Doughty, talking to a ship's carpenter, Edward Bright, confided that he thought the queen and her council were corrupt. Moreover, Doughty said, the mission's backers had ordered Drake to consult him on everything and that it was intended that he and Drake share authority.

The expedition finally got under way on December 13. By Christmas Day it was passing the northwest coast of Africa, and everyone aboard realized that the Mediterranean was not the destination. The nature of the voyage quickly became apparent. Heading for the Cape Verde Islands, Drake stopped Spanish and Portuguese ships along the way and confiscated their supplies for his own ships. He kept one ship, renaming it the *Christopher*.

At Cape Verde, the English captured a more valuable prize, the Portuguese *Santa Maria*. Drake not only appropriated the ship, renaming it the *Mary* and giving its captain the *Benedict* in return, but also took its highly skilled navigator, Nuño de Silva, along with his charts of the eastern coast of South America.

Trouble from Thomas Doughty

The long voyage to that coast came next. The fleet would be out of sight of land for more than 60 days. Such a long time, with many men together in cramped quarters, was a formula for dissension, and the man who brought it about was Thomas Doughty, whom Drake had made captain of the *Mary*.

The trouble arose over the Portuguese treasure still aboard the *Mary*. Cooke's account says that Doughty accused Drake's brother, Thomas, of stealing some of the goods. Another version claims that Doughty was the accused.

The treasure was not the only source of trouble. Drake heard complaints that Doughty had allowed the "gentlemen" to idle about while sailors did the heavy work. Drake's solution to both problems was to transfer Doughty to the *Pelican*, either as a subordinate or as captain, while he remained on the *Mary*.

The change of scenery did not help. On the *Pelican*, Doughty tried to enlist the aid of some of the crew, hinting that he might take over the ship, desert Drake, and go off on a raid of his own in the Caribbean. The tipping point occurred when Drake sent John Brewer, one of his favorite musicians, to the *Pelican* as a messenger. Brewer was the victim of a rough, crude practical joke that so enraged Drake that he ordered Doughty to come aboard the *Mary* to explain. Before Doughty could reach the deck, however, Drake, according to Cooke, shouted, "Stay there, Thomas Doughty, for I must send you to another place." He then ordered Doughty to be transferred to the *Swan* as a prisoner.

Such was the state of things when, on April 5, 1578, the ships reached the coast of Brazil. Storms, however, separated them and it was not until May 17 that they were reunited in a harbor at the Deseado River.

Confrontation

The last ship to appear was the *Swan*, and Drake soon learned that Doughty had continued to work against him, even while he was imprisoned. At one point Doughty had told Fletcher, the chaplain, that he would cause the crew to cut one another's throats. When the two men met, there was a furious argument. Doughty implied that Drake was a liar, whereupon Drake lost his temper, struck Doughty, and ordered him hauled bodily aboard the *Christopher* along with Doughty's brother John.

The ships remained in the Deseado Harbor for more than two weeks and on June 3 resumed their southward journey. Drake had decided to consolidate his ships, abandoning the *Swan* and *Christopher*, and proceeding with the *Pelican*, *Mary*, *Marigold*, and *Elizabeth*. The Doughty brothers were aboard the *Elizabeth*, watched closely by its captain, John Winter.

Two weeks later, they reached Port San Julian, the same spot where Magellan had stayed before venturing into the strait. Drake, likewise, wanted time to put things in order before following Magellan's route. The *Mary* had been so damaged by a storm that he decided to strip and abandon it and thus reduce his fleet to three ships. He also was determined that, before attempting the strait, he would settle the matter of what to do about Thomas Doughty.

On June 30 Drake gathered every man in the company to an island in the bay. According to Cooke's account, he confronted Doughty and accused him of working toward "the great hindrance and overthrow of this voyage" and said that, if convicted, "you have deserved death." When Doughty then said that he would be tried in England once the voyage ended, Drake refused, saying that the trial would be then and there.

Doughty was not a lawyer for nothing. He asked if Drake's commission from the queen permitted such a trial. When Drake answered that his commission was good enough, Doughty demanded to see it. Drake refused, had the defendant tied up, and quickly appointed a jury.

The Trial

Edward Bright was the primary witness, relating what Doughty had told him back in Plymouth and adding that Doughty had said that Lord Burghley knew the secret destination of the voyage. When Drake said that this could not be true, Doughty made what turned out to be a fatal mistake, saying, "He [Burghley] had it from me."

Drake seized on this slip. "Lo, my masters," he cried, "what this fellow hath done. . . . Her Majesty gave me special commandment that of all men that [Burghley] should not know it."

Doughty's friend Leonard Vicary tried to intervene, saying the trial was illegal. Drake would have none of it. "I have not to do with you crafty lawyers," he said, "neither care I for the law, but I know what I will do." At this point, the jury withdrew and found Doughty guilty.

Drake, however, sensed that some of his men questioned the legality of the trial. He led everyone except for the Doughty brothers to his tent where he went through some papers, searching for something that would support his claim. Finally, he said, "God's will! I have left in my cabin [on the *Pelican*] that I should especially have had." He showed the group various letters from such high-ranking personages as Hatton and Walsingham, but even Cooke wrote that he surely would have produced a royal commission if he had one.

Drake then asked the jury to determine punishment, making it clear that he did not think the voyage could proceed without Thomas Doughty's execution. He then asked the jurors to raise their hands if agreeing with him on the death penalty. All did so, but Cooke wrote that fear of Drake led to some of the votes.

The execution was scheduled for July 2, 1578. Doughty made out his will, and shared religious communion and even his final meal with Drake. He then asked the men to forgive him, embraced Drake, called him his "good Captain," and knelt before the executioner. When Doughty's head had been cut off, Drake held it up and said, "Lo! This is the end of traitors."

A Long Wait

Because of bad weather—July was midwinter in the Southern Hemisphere—Drake would have to wait another six weeks before setting out for the Strait of Magellan. He knew that some of his men resented Doughty's execution, and he was determined to clear the air. On August 11, Parson Fletcher administered communion to all hands and prepared to begin his

DRAKE'S SERMON

On August 11, 1578, shortly after the execution of Thomas Doughty for treason, Francis Drake called all his men together. When the chaplain, Francis Fletcher, rose to begin a sermon, Drake stopped him, saying, as quoted by John Cooke in Hampden's *Francis Drake: Privateer*, "Nay, soft, Master Fletcher, I must preach this day myself." And he went on to say,

> Thus it is, my masters, that we are very far from our country and friends; we are compassed in on every side with our enemies ... Wherefore we must have these mutinies and discords that are grown amongst us redressed, for by the life of God it doth even take my wits from me to think on it; here is such controversy between the sailors and the gentlemen, and such stomaching between the gentlemen and sailors, that it doth even make me mad to hear it. But, my masters, I must have it left [stopped], for I must have the gentlemen to hale and draw [work] with the mariner, and the mariner with the gentleman. What, let us show ourselves all to be of a company, and let us not give occasion to the enemy to rejoice at our decay and overthrow. I would know him that would refuse to set his hand to a rope, but I know there is not any such here ... Also if there be any here willing to return home let me understand of them ... but let them take heed that they go homeward, for if I find them in my way I will surely sink them.

No one accepted his offer.

sermon. Drake stopped him, saying—again from John Cooke's account of the voyage— "I must preach this day myself."

He had been angered, he said, by disagreements between the "gentlemen" and the ordinary sailors. From now on, he decreed, the gentlemen and sailors would labor side by side. If any of the company did not agree, he said, they could sail back to England in the *Marigold*. None chose to do so.

On August 20, the three ships reached the mouth of the strait. Drake had them dip their topsails as a salute to Queen Elizabeth, ordered a religious service, and then announced that the *Pelican* would henceforth be known as the *Golden Hind*. Under the new name—that of the golden dog that served as a symbol of his patron Christopher Hatton—the ship was to become one of the most famous in the history of navigation.

Two days later, a favorable northeasterly wind at their backs, the *Golden Hind*, the *Marigold*, and the *Elizabeth* entered the Strait of Magellan. Luck was with Drake. The wind stayed favorable and moderate, and the ships were able to make the 330-mile trip in only 16 days, a passage that had taken Magellan 37 days and would later take others almost 50 days. The water was calm enough for stops every so often to send rowboats ashore to gather penguins for food.

On September 6, the little fleet reached the last piece of land, Desolation Island. Drake had planned to erect a monument to Queen Elizabeth, but the weather was turning foul and he could only drop the monument into the surf, unable to land. He then led the way to where his countrymen had never been—the waters of the southern Pacific Ocean.

Around the World—Pacific

When Francis Drake's ships cleared the Strait of Magellan in September 1578, they found the Pacific Ocean to be little like a peaceful sea, which is the meaning of its name. As they tried to go north, fierce storms blew them back to the south.

Drake's maps showed the South American coast running northwest from the strait, whereas it actually runs almost due north. The Spaniards knew this but had not been willing to share their knowledge. So it was that Drake fruitlessly plowed northwest for two days before the storm hit. It was as if, according to *The World Encompassed*, "God by a contrary wind and intolerable tempest, seemed to set Himself against us."

The gale blew for more than a month, and the ships could do nothing except yield to it, being driven back to the south far below the strait. On September 30, the *Marigold* sank, killing all 29 men onboard. Fletcher claimed in his original narrative, as quoted in *The World Encompassed*, that he could

The *Golden Hind*, formerly called the *Pelican* and weighing about 100 tons, served Drake well. It was on this English galleon that Drake completed his voyage around the globe from 1577 to 1580. The ship returned to Plymouth Harbor with only 56 of the original 100 crew members onboard.

hear his comrades' "fearful cries when the hand of God came upon them."

On October 7 the *Golden Hind* and *Elizabeth* were able to claw their way back to shore near the mouth of the strait. They had hardly anchored, however, when the storm increased.

When the *Golden Hind's* anchor cable broke, Drake was forced out to sea, signaling to Captain Winter that he should remain.

When the *Golden Hind* did not reappear for three weeks, Winter decided to abandon the voyage and return home. Eight men died and two deserted at stops along the way, but the *Elizabeth* eventually reached England in June 1579. All Winter could report concerning Drake was that he had last been seen in a storm in the Pacific.

Meanwhile, Drake had not only weathered the storm but had also made an important discovery in the process. The *Golden Hind* was driven southward for almost three weeks, able to take refuge only occasionally among small islands that dotted the coast. Finally, according to Fletcher, as quoted by Sugden, it reached the "utmost island of Terra Incognito, to the southward of America, whereat we arriving, made both the seas to be one and the self same sea, and that there was no farther land beyond the heights of that island." The island Drake had reached was possibly Horn Island, the southernmost part of South America almost 400 miles from where he had exited the strait.

He had discovered, as he later told Hawkins, quoted in Kelsey's book, that Terra Incognito, as the land south of the Strait of Magellan was called, was not a continent, but "broken islands . . . compassed about with the sea on every side." Drake was not able to sail around the last island, but anchored on the west side and went overland alone to the southernmost tip. There, in a dramatic gesture, he stretched himself out on the ground so that he later could tell his crew that he had been further south "than any of them, yea, or any man as yet known."

It was evident to Drake that open sea lay south of the island, and that this open sea extended into the Atlantic Ocean. His discovery was not generally known until many years after his death, the English not wishing to give such information to rival nations. Eventually, however, it would make the voyage between the oceans much easier. Rounding Cape Horn, while still difficult for sailing ships, was at least much easier than the Strait of Magellan.

Doubts and Credit

Some historians and even some of Drake's contemporaries, however, doubt that he made such a discovery. One English mariner, Richard Madox, suggested in 1582 that Drake "found some kind of draft among the Portuguese or Spaniards and thus put forth their little commentaries as his own." Most authorities, however give Drake major credit for the discovery, and the body of water between the tip of South America and the northernmost Antarctic islands is still known as the Drake Passage.

On October 28, 1578, when the wind finally shifted, the *Golden Hind* was able to head north. Although Drake did not know the fates of the *Elizabeth* (which sailed on to England) and the *Marigold* (which had been swallowed by the ocean) and would continue to search for them, he was alone in the Pacific. Of the 170 men who had accompanied him from Plymouth, perhaps about 80 remained.

On November 25 the *Golden Hind* anchored near the island of Mocha off the coast of Chile. It was not a pleasant visit. The inhabitants, after an initial friendly greeting, attacked a lightly armed landing party. Two crewmen were captured and massacred and two more were mortally wounded by arrows, including the cimarrone Diego. Drake himself was hit twice, once just below the right eye.

Although there were two sizeable towns nearby, the English had suffered too many injuries to attack them. Instead, they sailed north, anchoring in a bay just north of Valparaiso, the port for the Chilean capital of Santiago. It was now that their luck, which had been uniformly bad since the strait, seemed to turn around. They found a native fisherman who hated the Spaniards so much that he was willing to guide the English into

Valparaiso. On December 5, enough of his men having recovered, Drake began his great Pacific raid.

The *La Capitana*

The *Golden Hind* slipped into the harbor after dark to find only one ship anchored, the *La Capitana*. Someone in Drake's crew knew enough Spanish to convince its crew that the newcomers were countrymen. By the time they knew otherwise, an armed boarding party had come over the side and the Spaniards were locked below.

The cargo of the *La Capitana* was a rich one—gold pesos, wine, and lumber, the last always useful to make ship repairs. The official report put the amount of gold pesos at 24,000, but it was likely much more. Drake and other privateers routinely failed to report all of their booty, holding back considerable amounts for themselves and their crews.

Perhaps more valuable were the ship's sailing master, Juan Griego, and his detailed charts of the western coast, not only of South America, but also of North America, as far north as San Diego, California. Both Griego and his charts were transferred to the *Golden Hind*.

Taking the captured ship with him, Drake then sailed north to Tongoy Bay. This was the spot at which the *Golden Hind*, *Elizabeth*, and *Marigold* were to have met if they became separated, but only Drake was there. He then kept moving north along the coast, stopping along the way to take on water and food, until he reached an isolated harbor. Safe from attack, he had the carpenters assemble a pinnace and repair the hull of the *Golden Hind*. He also brought his artillery out of storage, and when the ship was ready it boasted 18 guns, vastly more firepower than any Spanish ship in the Pacific.

Thus prepared, Drake worked his way northward. He raided the town of Puerto de Tarapacá and seized two ships at Arica, collecting about 50 bars of silver and a quantity of wine. Further north, he captured another ship and heard from its crew that there was a treasure ship belonging to San Juan de Anton a few miles up the coast at Callo, the port city of Peru's capital, Lima. He would find no great treasure in the several ships at Callo, but he got information just as valuable. The treasure ship, the *Nuestra Señora de la Concepcion*, had recently left Callo bound for Panama.

A Rich Prize

On Sunday, March 1, the intended victim was overtaken. When the *Golden Hind* sailed alongside the ship, Drake shouted, according to Hampden's book, "You must strike your sails in the name of the queen of England." When Anton challenged him to come do it himself, Drake opened fire. One of Anton's masts was splintered in two by a cannonball, and several Spaniards, included Anton, were wounded. A moment later, Englishmen swarmed aboard and the battle was over.

The *Nuestra Señora de la Concepcion* would turn out to be one of the richest prizes of Drake's career. Onboard were 80 pounds of gold, 13 chests of silver coins, and an assortment of jewels. There were 26 tons of silver bars, so many that Anton had tossed out the stones normally used as extra weight in the hold to keep the ship stable and had used the precious metal instead. Anton's official estimate of the prize's value was 362,000 pesos, roughly the equivalent of $30 million in current U.S. dollars.

During the six days it took to transfer the loot to the *Golden Hind*, Drake was a friendly host to his captives. When he was finished, he distributed gifts, including a German musket and a gilded breastplate for Anton, about 30 pesos each to members of his crew, and assorted goods ranging from tar to ladies' fans.

After crossing the Strait of Magellan, Drake sailed north along the Pacific coast of South America. He attacked Spanish ports and towns and plundered Spanish ships. The *Golden Hind* overtook the Spanish galleon *Nuestra Señora de la Concepción*, which had onboard loot worth more than 360,000 pesos, the largest treasure captured to that date.

Drake did not need any more loot to make the voyage a triumph, but he would not turn down any that came his way. While the *Golden Hind* was beached for a week at Caño Island off the coast of Costa Rica, the pinnace seized a merchant ship. A week later, near Sonssonate in El Salvador, he took another ship, which yielded rich cloth and chests of Chinese porcelain.

A Picture of Drake

The latter ship's owner, Don Francisco de Zárate, did not provide much in the way of treasure, but his subsequent report gives the most vivid picture of Francis Drake in his true element as a pirate captain. He described his captor as being about 35 years old, of medium height, thickset, and having a red beard. "He treats all his men with affection," Zárate wrote, as quoted by Bradford, "and they treat him with respect."

Drake worked alongside his men, as he had decreed months before in his speech after Doughty's execution, but there was no doubt as to his authority. When a ship was captured, no one "dared to take anything without his orders" and he "punished the least fault." Men removed their caps before speaking to him. He dined, to the accompaniment of musicians and from silver plates, with his officers, but no one could sit until Drake was seated. He liked to impress the captains of captured ships, inviting them to dine with him and boasting of his connection with Queen Elizabeth. "He took very little from me," Zárate concluded. "In fact he was very polite."

On April 15, about a week after releasing Zárate, Drake ended his historic raid at the Guatemalan port of Guatulco. His men sacked the town, taking 7,000 pesos in gold and goods from the home of a wealthy landowner and then stripped the church of everything of value. As they had in other Roman Catholic churches along the way, the Protestant Englishmen smashed crucifixes and statues of saints and used altar cloths to wipe their hands. There are few records, however, of Drake's men seriously harming a priest.

On April 16, 1579, Drake sailed away from Guatulco, leaving behind Nuño da Silva, the Portuguese pilot whom he had captured shortly after the voyage began. The Spaniards had seen the last of him, but did not realize it. Towns up and down the coast were warned to stay alert.

The Strait of Anian

At the same time, Spanish officials were trying to guess what Drake's eventual route back to England might be. Most thought Drake would cross the Pacific. He had hinted to Silva as much, adding that he was not afraid of being pursued. While that route was the one Drake eventually chose, he appears to have attempted another—the fabled but undiscovered Strait of Anian across the top of North America. If he did so—and some historians have claimed that this part of the voyage has been fabricated—it was a rare instance of Drake exploring for its own sake with no thought of loot.

According to *The World Encompassed*, the *Golden Hind* and one of the recently captured Spanish ships sailed about 4,200 miles up the coast, no doubt stopping frequently to take on food and water. When on June 3, 1579, they reached 42 degrees north in latitude—roughly parallel with the northern border of California—the weather turned "nipping cold." They continued north, reaching—according to the account—48 degrees, about on level with Vancouver Island in Canada.

The cold grew so intense that ropes and pulleys froze and it took six men to perform what three had done before. Meat, "as soon as it was removed from the fire, would presently in a manner be frozen up." Every hill was "covered with snow." This description is one reason for doubting the story. The weather at that latitude in June would have been much warmer.

Drake found that the coastline, instead of receding eastward toward a passage across the continent, ran ever-more westward. He guessed that "the Asian and American continent, which . . . if they be not fully joined, yet seem they to come very near one to the other." If this was the case, then "there is no passage at all through these northern coasts . . . or if there be, that yet it is un-navigable."

Landing in California

Forced to retreat, Drake sailed south until on June 17 he found a harbor described as being at 38 degrees, 30 minutes. This is in the vicinity of San Francisco Bay, but extensive research has failed to pinpoint the site. The most likely candidate, however, because of geographical features that match the description, is Drake's Bay, located at a point off the coast of present-day Marin County.

The weather here was more hospitable, and the inhabitants were friendly as well. The description of them in *The World Encompassed* has led anthropologists to believe that they were of the Miwok tribe. Drake, however, took no chances, ordering his men to build a fort in which they could defend themselves from any attack. As the days went by it was evident that there was little to fear. Indeed, the Miwok seemed to think that these Europeans, the first they had seen, were either gods or spirits of the dead returned to earth.

The Miwok might have even asked Drake to be their ruler. On June 26, the entire tribe progressed down a hill to the English camp. Several men then made speeches indicating to the Englishmen, according to *The World Encompassed*, that they wished Drake "to take up the province and kingdom into his hand." They set a crown of feathers on his head and hung chains made of clamshells around his neck.

Drake was up to the occasion. Delivering an oration of his own, whereby he "in the name . . . of Her Most Excellent Majesty [Queen Elizabeth] . . . took up sceptre, crown, and dignity of the said country into his hand." Indeed, Drake claimed the entire area for England, naming it New Albion for the "white banks and cliffs which lie toward the sea." He ordered a plaque bearing the queen's name, the date, and a coin bearing Elizabeth's likeness to be nailed to a "great and firm post."

THE NOVA ALBION PLAQUE

After claiming New Albion, as he named the area he visited on the California coast, for England and Queen Elizabeth, Drake, in the words of *The World Encompassed*, set up "a plate of brass fast nailed to a great and firm post, whereon is engraven Her Grace's [Elizabeth's] name, and the day and year of our arrival there, and of the free giving up of the province and kingdom."

In 1936 a store clerk named Beryle Shinn claimed to have found near San Francisco Bay a brass plaque bearing a date of June 17, 1579, and claiming "Nova Albion" for England. The California Historical Society paid Shinn $3,500 for the plaque, but then another man—William Caldeira—claimed to have found the plaque and, thinking it had no value, discarded it near where Shinn claimed to have found it.

Scholarly opinion went back and forth for decades as to the authenticity of the plaque, but in 1977 analyses of the metal and the carving showed it to be a fake.

When it was time for the Englishmen to depart, the Miwok "took a sorrowful farewell of us." The Spanish ship was left behind, and the *Golden Hind* set out alone. The Miwok ran to the top of the hills so as to keep the ship in view as long as possible.

Across the Pacific

The journey across the Pacific was uneventful but very long—68 days without sight of land. On September 30 an island, probably Palau east of the Philippine Islands, was sighted. After stopping there to trade with the natives, Drake landed at the island of Mindanao in the Philippines, then headed southwest toward the Moluccas and the Celebes Islands, famed for their spices and a source of rich trade with Europe.

Drake reached the Moluccas on November 3 and remained there for a week, restocking his ship and engaging in a bit of international diplomacy. The ruling sultan, Babur, had driven the Portuguese from most of his realm after they had murdered his father. When Drake arrived, the Portuguese were trying to regain control. Babur reasoned that England could not only help him against the Portuguese, but could take their place as a trading partner.

Drake and Babur agreed that, in exchange for the spice trade, England within two years would send a fleet to the sultan's aid. The two men exchanged gifts, and six tons of valuable cloves were packed into the hold of the already crowded *Golden Hind*. No military aid was ever received, but trading nevertheless continued until Spain took over the Moluccas in 1606. As late as 1605, Babur's son was still looking for English ships, writing to King James I and referring, as quoted by Bradford, to the promise of "the great Captain, Francis Drake."

The next stop was an uninhabited island near the Celebes. Water, game, and fruit were plentiful, and Drake remained there almost a month, taking an opportunity to attend to the *Golden Hind's* hull once more and giving his men a chance to rest. With both ship and crew fit, he resumed the journey on December 12, 1579. Four weeks later, it almost came to a sudden and tragic end.

On the Reef

The *Golden Hind* was trying to find a passage south of the Celebes into the Indian Ocean when it struck a submerged reef near Peleng Island and was held fast. Fortunately, the hull had not been breached but, unless the ship could be freed, it would eventually be pounded to pieces by the waves. The treasure would be lost and so, perhaps, would be many lives.

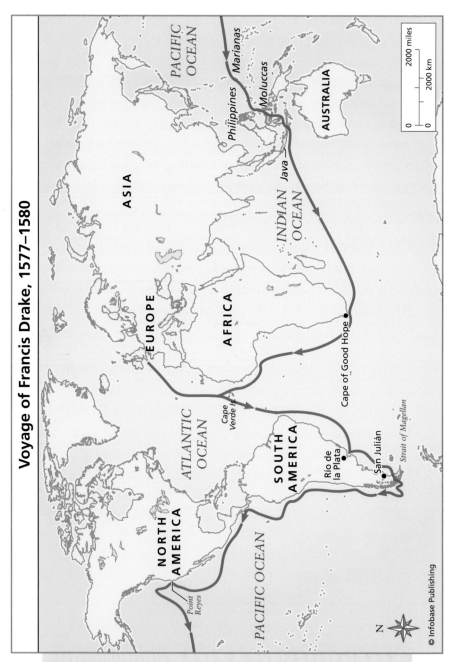

Voyage of Francis Drake, 1577–1580

On September 26, 1580, the *Golden Hind* sailed into Plymouth with Drake and his reduced crew, along with a cargo of rich spices and Spanish treasures. With this expedition, Drake became the second man to sail around the world, and the first Englishman to do so.

Drake tried to use a small boat to drop an anchor from the *Golden Hind* at some distance so that the ship could be winched free, but there was no firm bottom. The ship was lightened as much as possible. Among the cargo thrown overboard were three tons of the recently acquired cloves. Now, according to *The World Encompassed*, there was "nothing to trust to but prayers and tears." Finally, as if in answer, the wind changed direction, shoved the ship off the reef, and "made us glad men."

It took more than a month longer to find a way through the islands into the Indian Ocean, but by early March 1580 the *Golden Hind* was at the west coast of Java. Drake spent two weeks there, then headed west, coming in sight of the African coast on May 21. He rounded the Cape of Good Hope in June, stopped in Sierra Leone for water, then headed north for England.

The *Golden Hind* reached the entrance to Plymouth Sound on September 26, 1580. It had been gone 90 days short of three years. Of the original party of about 175 men, only 56 remained. Drake had done what no other sailor had accomplished, sailing his own ship around the world. Not only had he returned, but with a vast treasure. The question, however, was what kind of welcome would he receive.

Fame
and Fortune

His voyage around the word made Francis Drake one of the richest and most famous men in England. His name was on the lips of everyone from royal palace to dockside pub. He became a country gentleman and entered politics on the local and national levels. But Drake on land was like a fish out of water, and it would not be too many years before he set out on another adventure.

When he first arrived back at Plymouth, however, he did not know if he would be treated as a hero or a criminal. Before entering the harbor, the *Golden Hind* hailed a fishing boat, asking if Queen Elizabeth was still alive. Only when told that she was still on the throne and in good health did Drake proceed.

He learned that in his absence Philip of Spain had grown stronger than ever. He had been recognized as king of Portugal earlier in the year. His troops were strengthening their control on the Netherlands and were helping a rebellion against the English in Ireland. Although neither ruler wanted it, Spain and England were drifting closer to war.

To get an idea of how his return might be viewed, Drake sent a messenger to London. The initial reply was that the queen was displeased and that the treasure might need to be returned. This, however, was only the official version intended to reach Spanish ears. Elizabeth sent a private message to Drake telling him not to worry and ordering him to come to London.

Private Interview

When Drake arrived, he was ushered into the queen's presence for a private interview that lasted six hours. There is no record of their conversation, but he very likely said that much of what he had taken had not been officially registered, leaving Spain with no way of knowing the total. Elizabeth promptly canceled an order to have the treasure inventoried and stored in the Tower of London. Instead, she directed Drake to deliver his loot for safekeeping, but not before he had—with no witnesses or accounting—subtracted £10,000 for himself. He later wrote that he took £10,000 for himself and another £14,000 for his crew, but he probably took much more.

The full total of Drake's plunder was never known, but estimates ranged as high as £600,000, the equivalent of $165 million in U.S. dollars today. Those who had invested in the voyage were said to have made a profit of 4,700 percent.

The Spaniards were furious, but when their ambassador demanded an explanation, he was told one would be considered when Spain explained what its troops were doing in Ireland. Furthermore, he was told, the queen had conducted a thorough investigation and had concluded Drake had done no damage to Spain.

Despite the friction between England and Spain, caused by Drake's plunders on the high seas, Queen Elizabeth walked aboard the *Golden Hind* and awarded Drake a knighthood. Drake presented the queen with a jeweled ship commemorating the circumnavigation, and the queen gave him a jewel with her portrait, an uncommon gift to a commoner.

Sir Francis

Elizabeth went out of her way to indicate her approval of his actions. At her command, the *Golden Hind* was brought to London so that she could visit Drake on board. So many people accompanied her that when they tried to follow her across a plank bridge to the ship, the bridge collapsed, sending dozens of richly dressed courtiers into the Thames River mud.

SPENDING SPREE

The treasure captured on Drake's voyage around the world made him one of the richest men in England. He made the most of his wealth, buying property, marrying an heiress, and distributing expensive presents. Spain's ambassador to England, Bernardino de Mendoza, described Drake's spending in a report to King Philip, as quoted in *Sir Francis Drake* by John Sugden:

> Drake is squandering more money than any man in England, and proportionately, all those who came with him are doing the same. He gave to the Queen the crown which I described in a former letter as having been made here. She wore it on New Year's Day. It has in it five emeralds, three of them almost as long as a little finger, whilst the two round ones are valued at 20,000 crowns, coming, as they do, from Peru. He has also given the Queen a diamond cross as a New Year's gift, as is the custom here, of the value of 5,000 crowns. . . . The Chancellor [Christopher Hatton] got eight hundred crowns worth of silver plate, and all the councilors and secretaries had a share in a similar form, Leicester getting most of all. The Queen shows extraordinary favour to Drake, and never fails to speak to him when she goes out in public, conversing with him for a long time.

After a tour of the ship and a sumptuous banquet, the queen took a golden sword and ordered Drake to kneel before her. The king of Spain, she joked, had asked her to cut off Drake's head. Instead, she gave the sword to the French ambassador and told him to perform the ceremony making the former Devon farm boy a knight of the realm.

Drake played the part fully. He was a familiar presence at the court and could frequently be seen strolling though gardens while chatting with the queen. He gave lavish presents, particularly to the queen. A contemporary historian, John Stow, wrote, as quoted in *Sir Francis Drake* by Peter Whitfield, that "his name and fame became admirable in all places."

He was not admired by everyone, however. Richard Madox, quoted in John Cummins's article in *History Today*, referred to him sarcastically as "our golden knight." Some aristocratic members of the court regarded him as an upstart at best and as a criminal at worst. Lord Sussex, hearing Drake boast of his exploits at a dinner, remarked that capturing a lightly armed ship with a superior warship was hardly anything to brag about. And Lord Burghley, who thoroughly disapproved of Drake, flatly refused a New Year's present of 10 bars of gold, saying he could not, in good conscience, accept stolen goods.

Buckland Abbey

This lack of respect was evident when Drake sought to buy a manor house worthy of his recently acquired title and wealth. Only four miles from Plymouth stood Buckland Abbey, built in the 1200s by monks, taken away from them in 1539 by King Henry VIII, and turned into a mansion by the Grenville family.

The house was bought, along with much of its furnishings and about 500 acres of land, for £3,400. It was not sold, however, to Drake, but to two middlemen, Christopher Harris and John Hele. Only after the deal was completed did Richard Grenville discover that the buyer had grown up the son of a nearby tenant farmer. Drake did not stop with the purchase of Buckland Abbey. Queen Elizabeth gave him the manor of Sherford, and he bought two others—Yarcombe and Stampford Spinney.

How Drake's wife, Mary, reacted to her new status as Lady Drake is not known. Presumably, she served as hostess at some of the gatherings at her husband's various homesteads, but there is no record. At any rate, she was not to enjoy her newfound wealth long as she died from unknown causes in January 1583.

Drake would marry again two years later, this time to Elizabeth Sydenham, daughter and heiress of Sir George Sydenham. She was in her twenties and extremely attractive. She was wealthy as well. In time she would inherit and bring into the marriage three more manors and nine tracts of land scattered throughout southeastern England.

Property in Plymouth

Drake was not content only to be a country squire. He bought 40 separate properties in Plymouth, including 29 houses, 4 gardens, 2 stables, and 5 warehouses. His holdings made him the largest landowner in the city except for the Hawkins family and the city government itself.

Such a prominent citizen should be recognized, and Plymouth did so by selecting him as its mayor in September 1581. It must have been a largely ceremonial position, or at least Drake seems to have considered it so. His sole accomplishment, according to city records, was to cause a compass to be set up on the Hoe, a public park.

Drake was slightly more active on the national scene as a member of parliament, England's legislative body. He entered parliament early in 1581, and while there is no record of any activity on his part during this term, his second term, which began in 1584, was different. He served on two committees, one concerning the prohibition of sports on Sundays and the other dealing with fishing. He was probably much more interested in his third assignment, a committee on legislation that directed Walter Raleigh to establish an English colony in Virginia.

He was also constantly consulted on matters concerning the Royal Navy. His old shipmate, John Hawkins, had been made treasurer of the navy, and Drake served on what amounted to an advisory committee along with mariners Raleigh, Martin Frobisher, and Fulk Greville.

Speculation

Ever since his return from the voyage around the world, however, there had been intense speculation as to when and where his next mission would be. Spain's King Philip was especially worried. He wrote to his ambassador in England, as quoted by Sugden, "Tell me what has become of Drake and what you hear of arming of ships . . . It is important that I should know all about this."

Several possible missions were suggested, but it would be 1584 before one took shape. Early in the year, Drake was put in charge of assembling a fleet to go to the Moluccas. The investors included the queen, Sir Francis Walsingham, the earl of Leicester, and John Hawkins. Preparations dragged on so long, however, that the entire focus of the expedition changed.

That change was provided by King Philip himself. In May 1585 he suddenly ordered all English vessels in Spanish ports seized. The resulting uproar forced Queen Elizabeth to take action. She promised to intervene on behalf of the Dutch in the Netherlands, and she gave Drake a royal commission ordering him to raid Spanish ports and rescue English ships and sailors. Furthermore, he was free to raid Spanish ports or shipping at his pleasure to get money to repay those whose ships had been lost.

By September a fleet of more than 20 ships had been assembled. Drake was in overall command, and his captains included five men who had been around the world with him. Other prominent members of the expedition were Martin Frobisher, Richard and William Hawkins—son and nephew of John Hawkins—and Francis Knollys, Leicester's brother-in-law and a relative of the queen's. Christopher Carleill, an experienced soldier and also Walsingham's stepson, commanded not only a ship, but also the more than 1,000 land troops assigned to the expedition.

The Fleet Sails

The fleet sailed on September 14 and headed straight for the port of Vigo on the northwest coast of Spain. The local governor was in no position to offer resistance. The English ships, he told Drake, had already been freed, but he agreed to furnish the fleet with extra supplies provided the town was spared.

When the fleet left on October 11, Spanish officials were in a panic. They had no idea where Drake would strike next. All Philip could do was order his naval commander, the marquis of Santa Cruz, to defend the Spanish coast and order ships due to leave for the West Indies to stay in port. As for any treasure fleet already bound for Spain, all Philip could do was hope Drake could not find it.

That is exactly what happened. Drake had stayed so long in Vigo that one treasure fleet arrived elsewhere while he was still there. A second fleet left the Azores on October 7 and was headed for Spain just as Drake was on an intersecting course toward the Canary Islands. The two fleets sailed past one another out of sight, neither one realizing how close they had been.

Having found that almost all the impounded English ships had been freed, Drake had set out for the West Indies. The weather was so bad in the Canary Islands, where he stopped on the way, that the fleet moved on to the Cape Verde Islands. There, Drake attempted to take the town of Santa Cruz on the

Isle of Palma, but encountered stiff resistance. He had only a little more luck elsewhere, capturing three other towns but getting little in the way of plunder.

More Bad Luck

Drake's ill fortune continued after the voyage across the Atlantic continued. A disease, possibly typhus, swept through the fleet. Upwards of 300 men died and many were so ill they could not function. When Drake reached the West Indies, he had to put in at an uninhabited island for a few weeks.

Once the disease had receded and his ships were cleansed, Drake began his raid. The first target was Santo Domingo on the island of Hispaniola. Before dawn on New Year's Day 1586, Drake secretly landed a large force under Carleill's command up the coast from the city. He then rejoined the fleet and sailed to the city harbor. The Spaniards, thinking to prevent a landing, sent troops out of the city gates toward the shore. At that point, Carleill's soldiers appeared, advancing on them from two directions. The Spaniards tried to retreat into the city, but it was too late and the city was quickly in English hands.

In calculating potential profits for the voyage, Drake had hoped to wring 500,000 ducats, about $10 million in today's money, from Santo Domingo. He was to be disappointed, having vastly overestimated the city's wealth. The royal treasury yielded only about 16,000 ducats, and he would have to get the remainder by holding the entire city for ransom. He started by demanding one million ducats, but eventually had to settle for an additional 25,000 before sailing on.

Officials throughout Spain and its empire could only guess where Drake would hit next. Rumors placed him everywhere from Havana to the coast of Portugal, but his next target was Cartagena.

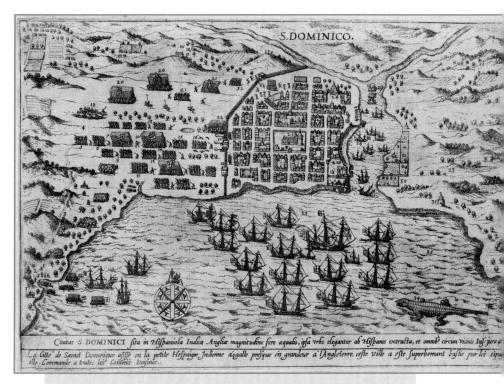

S.DOMINICO.

Ciuitas S.DOMINICI sita in Hispaniola India Anglie magnitudine fere aequalis, ipsa vrbs eleganter ab Hispanis extructa, et omnib᷑ circum vicinis Insꞏ jura a

La Cité de Sainct Dominique asisse en la petite Hespaigne Indienne aegalle presque en grandeur a'l'Angleterre, ceste ville a este superbement bastie par les espa elle . Commande a toutes les᷑ Contrées Voisines..

In 1586, Drake attacked Santo Domingo, the largest city in what is now the Dominican Republic. The men approached from two directions and easily captured the city. The royal treasury was able to raise only part of the profits Drake demanded, and he held the city for ransom for more ducats. Following Drake's invasion, the capital was abandoned and left to the mercy of pirates. Above is the plan of Drake's attack on Santo Domingo.

The Taking of Cartagena

On the night of February 9, Carleill and 1,000 soldiers landed on the tip of a narrow neck of land extending south from the city and enclosing the inner harbor. While they made their way through the marsh, Drake sailed as close as he could to the harbor, firing his guns. Just before dawn, Carleill attacked, quickly storming a barricade and chasing the fleeing Spaniards into the city.

Drake treated Cartagena much the same as he had Santo Domingo. He seized 5,000 ducats from the governor and demanded a ransom of 400,000 ducats from the city. When the governor proclaimed this amount impossible, Drake ordered his men to begin a systematic destruction of the city. The governor yielded, but 107,000 ducats were all that could be raised.

Drake was undecided on his next move. He had seized treasure worth more than £60,000—a considerable sum, but still far short of what it had taken to finance the voyage. There were other tempting targets, such as Havana and Panama, but the voyage was far behind schedule and so many men had been lost to disease —another 100 at Cartagena—that success was doubtful. Also, he had heard a fleet of Spanish warships was on the way. When his captains suggested that they end the raid and head for England, Drake agreed.

Raid on Florida

There would, however, be one more conquest. After a brief stop for water in Cuba, the fleet anchored off the coast of St. Augustine, Florida. It was by no means a wealthy place, but Drake thought it might pose a threat to Walter Raleigh's new colony up the coast in Roanoke, Virginia. On May 28, he captured the town, taking money worth £2,000 and all the artillery pieces.

On June 9, Drake reached Roanoke. The colony was not doing well. Expected supplies from England had not arrived, and the natives were growing more hostile. Drake offered the governor, Ralph Lane, food and one of his ships with which the colonists could search for a friendlier site. When the ship was damaged by a storm, however, Lane elected to return to England with Drake along with all the remaining colonists.

Drake arrived in England on July 27, 1586. He boasted to Burghley, as quoted by Sugden, that "there is now a very great gap opened very little to the liking of the King of Spain." The voyage, however, had been a financial failure. Drake's backers would eventually receive back only about three-fourths of what they had invested. But what came to be known as the Great Raid had important consequences. Spain was thoroughly alarmed at what Drake had done, and even the usually reserved Burghley said, as quoted by Bradford, "Sir Francis Drake is a fearful man to the King of Spain."

King Philip, in fact, had been pushed to the limit by Drake's raid, along with the incursion of English troops in the Netherlands. A royal secretary wrote in February 1587, as quoted by Sugden, "defensive methods are not enough to cover everything, but forces us to apply the fire in their [England's] homeland." To apply this fire, the largest fleet the world had ever seen was assembled. It would be known as the Spanish Armada.

The Armada

By 1586, King Philip of Spain, having endured England as a thorn in his side for more than 20 years, decided to pull it out once and for all. In what he called the Enterprise of England, he would invade and conquer the island nation, adding it to his immense empire and restoring the Roman Catholic Church. His chief instrument for doing so was a massive fleet—the Spanish Armada. In its way, their nation's freedom on the line, stood Sir Francis Drake and the Royal Navy.

The Armada was never intended to carry an invading army—far too many ships would be needed to transport men, horses, and artillery such a distance. Rather the plan was for the Armada to sail to the Netherlands, defeat the Royal Navy along the way if the opportunity arose, and then to escort barges the few miles across the English Channel carrying the Spanish army commanded by the duke of Parma. The English did know such details and had to be prepared to confront the

In 1588, Spain was the most powerful country in the world and had a massive fleet to protect it. The Spanish Armada, however, represented the old tradition of naval warfare, using the ships to fight as if on land, boarding enemy ships, and conducting hand-to-hand combat. Spanish ships rode high out of the water and their height made them awkward to sail. English ships were race built, sailing lower in the water and closer to the wind, making them faster and more maneuverable.

Armada in case it attempted to land an army anywhere along the southern coast.

Drake did not want to wait on the Spanish fleet. Instead, he argued for an immediate attack on Spanish ports to try to destroy the ships before they even sailed. He wrote to Queen Elizabeth, as quoted by Bradford, "The advantage of time and place in all martial actions is half a victory."

Drake's Instructions

The queen, despite her usual caution, agreed. In December 1586 Drake received instructions, as quoted by Bradford, "to impeach the provisions of Spain" and to "distress the ships within the havens [ports] themselves." Accordingly, Drake mustered a fleet of 23 ships with about 2,000 men. It sailed on April 2, 1587, Drake having written to Walsingham, as quoted by Sugden, that "The wind commands me away."

Off the northwest corner of Spain, Drake learned that a great number of ships were concentrated at the Spanish port of Cadiz about 50 miles (80 km) northwest of the Strait of Gibraltar. He arrived there on April 19 and, to Vice Admiral William Borough's horror, immediately took advantage of a favoring wind to sail directly into the outer harbor, signaling the rest of the fleet to follow.

Some 60 ships were anchored there, but they were not entirely unprotected. At least 10 oar-powered galleys were present, and their maneuverability inside the confined area should have given them the advantage. But the range of the English guns was longer and the galleys, after taking a broadside or two, fled to the safety of the inner harbor.

The captains and crews of the remaining ships were panic-stricken. Some vessels ran aground while attempting to escape. Others were simply abandoned. A ship from Genoa attempted to fight and was sunk. On shore, 26 people were crushed in a stampede to take shelter in a castle guarding the harbor.

With the sun now setting, Borough urged Drake to withdraw back to the open sea. Drake would have none of it. Instead he turned his men loose among the defenseless ships, looting and burning. By nightfall the entire outer harbor was illuminated by blazing ships.

More Damage

This destruction still was not enough for Drake. He would not risk his larger ships in the inner harbor but instead led a group of small boats inside. His immediate target was a huge warship belonging to Admiral Santa Cruz himself. It was shortly a mass of flames as were other ships nearby.

All the next day the English continued to plunder and destroy. The duke of Medina Sidonia led his troops to the city, but all they could do was watch. One witness, quoted by Sugden, said the harbor resembled "a huge volcano, or something out of Hell . . . A sad and dreadful sight."

On the morning of April 21, Drake withdrew. He took four Spanish ships with him and left behind the remains of 34 more—31 burned and 3 sunk. In addition to crippling the Armada's preparation, he had inflicted considerable damage on Spain's national pride. It was bad enough to have endured raids on one's overseas possessions, but Drake had sailed into a major harbor in Spain itself and left it a smoking ruin.

He was by no means through. He sailed across the Gulf of Cadiz to Cape St. Vincent at the southwest corner of Portugal. From a base there he could intercept ships along the coast and those going to and from the Mediterranean. Borough, who had hung back from the fighting at Cadiz and urged some of his fellow captains to do the same, now wrote Drake a long letter advising him against the strategy. Drake, seeing perhaps another Doughty, immediately relieved Borough of his command and confined him to his cabin. At first it appeared as if Borough was right when an attack against the port town of Lagos failed, but a few miles down the coast Drake personally led an overland attack that captured four forts at Sagres on the tip of Cape St. Vincent.

Other targets had more military value. More than 40 ships were seized and their cargos destroyed. Also destroyed were more than 50 fishing boats and their nets. This deprived some fishermen of their livelihood, but it also meant fewer fish for the Armada.

On to Lisbon

When he had done as much damage as possible at Cape St. Vincent, Drake went north to Lisbon, in Portugal, where he knew the bulk of the Armada was being assembled. The harbor was far too well guarded for him to repeat his feat at Cadiz, but he blockaded the port for two days, much to the embarrassment of King Philip and Santa Cruz.

He might have stayed at Lisbon longer, but word reached him that there were some rich ships for the taking to the east of Lisbon near the Azores. The lure of treasure proved irresistible, and Drake yielded to it. On June 8, off the island of São Miguel, he captured the *San Felipe*, a huge East Indies merchant ship and the personal property of King Philip. He took his prize back to England, reaching Plymouth on June 26, and it took 17 ships to carry its cargo, valued at £112,000, to London.

Santa Cruz implored Philip to delay the Armada, but the king was determined. The admiral worked feverishly to rebuild what had been lost, but Santa Cruz worked himself to death, dying of exhaustion on February 9, 1588.

Philip had been aware of Santa Cruz's ill health and was prepared to name a successor. The successor, however, was unprepared for such a task and said so. The duke of Medina Sidonia protested that he had no experience with ships and, indeed, was prone to seasickness. Philip would not be moved.

Medina Sidonia might have been no sailor, but he was a brilliant administrator. By April 25 the Armada was in such a state of readiness that an elaborate blessing ceremony was conducted in the Lisbon cathedral. Medina Sidonia knelt at the altar to embrace a huge banner that had received the pope's blessing.

Lord Howard

Drake, meanwhile, argued for another attack. Elizabeth would not go that far, but she did send the navy's eastern squadron to join Drake's western squadron at Plymouth in order to have a larger force ready. The supreme commander, however, was not Drake, but Lord Howard of Effingham, a veteran sailor and the queen's cousin. There were at least two good reasons for this appointment. First, command of such a large fleet, according to the customs of the time, went to a member of the nobility. Second, some of the senior captains, such as John Hawkins and Martin Frobisher, might have refused to serve under Drake, whom they regarded as an equal.

While Drake and Howard fretted at Plymouth, pleading to be allowed to sail, the Armada sailed down the Tagus River from Lisbon and turned north toward the English Channel. It consisted of 151 ships, at least 72 of them prime warships with the rest made up of cargo vessels and small boats similar to pinnaces.

The voyage got off to a bad start. The rough Atlantic Ocean waves were too much for four galleys, which had to return to port. The rest struggled up the coast against a strong north wind. Seventeen ships were separated from the fleet and eventually returned to Lisbon. On June 19, having reached only the northwest corner of Spain, the remainder of the Armada had already used up so many supplies that it had to harbor at Corunna in northwestern Spain.

This was an open invitation to Drake. With Howard he urged Elizabeth to approve an attack, which she finally did. On July 17 the English sailed from Plymouth, but strong winds from the south forced them to return only five days later.

The Armada Sights England

Those same winds enabled the Armada to leave Corunna and head for the English Channel, coming in view of the Lizard, as the southwest tip of England is called. The English were on their guard. Pinnaces and other smaller ships had been patrolling the channel. One of them, captained by Thomas Fleming,

BOWLING ON PLYMOUTH HOE

Perhaps the most famous of all stories connected to Drake is that of Thomas Fleming, the sailor who first spotted the Spanish Armada and rushed to Plymouth with the news. There, he found Drake and Lord Howard bowling on the Hoe, a grassy area overlooking the harbor. After hearing Fleming blurt out his news, Drake is supposed to have said, as quoted in Ernle Bradford's *The Wind Commands Me*, "There is time enough to finish the game, and beat the Spaniards, too."

Whether Drake actually made such a comment has never been proved. The bowling story first appeared in 1624 in a Spanish pamphlet and was said to have been told by people old enough to have witnessed the event. But that pamphlet, even though mentioning the bowling game, says nothing about any comment by Drake. It was another century before the first recorded printing of Drake's statement.

Some military historians have argued that his comment makes no sense, because no time was to be wasted getting the English fleet out of Plymouth Harbor. Others say that it only would have been necessary for Drake and Howard to issue the orders, knowing the tide would not be favorable for an actual departure until about 10 P.M.

Another interesting, and factual, part of the story is that the name of Fleming's pinnace was the *Golden Hind*, named for the ship Drake had sailed around the world.

saw the huge expanse of sails in the distance. He knew it must be the Armada and raced back to Plymouth.

The story, never authenticated, is that—running to deliver the message to Drake and Howard—he found them bowling on Plymouth Hoe. Drake is supposed to have said, as quoted by Kelsey, "There is time enough to finish the game and beat the Spaniards, too."

Regardless of whether or not they finished the game, Drake and Howard most certainly would have ordered the fleet to make ready to sail. To be trapped inside Plymouth Harbor would have been a disaster. At 10 p.m. the English ships began leaving the harbor and by the next morning were heading west toward the Armada.

When the English came into Medina Sidonia's view on the eastern horizon late in the day, he was glad to see that he had the "weather gauge," meaning that the wind was at his back, giving him much more maneuverability in battle. He did not want to pass the English in the dark, thus giving them benefit of the west wind, and so anchored his fleet. He was stunned the next morning to find his opponents behind him, the wind at their back, having circled the Armada during the night.

The First Battle

If Medina Sidonia was surprised, so must the English have been to see such a vast number of ships facing them. The English actually had more ships, 197, but most were supply ships and pinnaces. In terms of fighting ships, the two sides were about equal, the English having 62 to the Armada's 72, although Spain's were larger.

The Armada was in the formation it was to hold through-out the series of battles—a crescent with the points on each side pointing toward the enemy. The English attacked, with Howard on the south end and Drake on the north. As the battle progressed, two things became clear. The English ships, race built, or much longer in relation to their width, were swifter and more maneuverable. The larger Spanish ships tried to close in and grapple with them, but were unable to do so. The English, in keeping their distance, did not get close enough to where their guns were able to inflict serious damage.

Such serious damage as there was happened after the firing stopped. The Spanish *Rosario* collided with another ship and lost her bowsprit, the spar to which the foremast was fastened, and some forward sails. A short time later, there was a tremendous explosion. Fire had broken out on the Spanish *San Salvador* and had reached the magazine where gunpowder was stored. The ship managed to stay afloat but was lost to the fleet.

When night fell, the Armada continued eastward in formation. Howard wanted to ensure he stayed near the enemy. He ordered Drake in the *Revenge* to lead the way and to hang a light in the stern, or rear, to act as a beacon for the rest of the fleet.

During the night, the light disappeared. Toward dawn, Howard thought he saw a light ahead and hurried to catch up. When it was light enough to see, he found that he had sailed almost into the middle of the Armada. Drake was nowhere to be seen.

Drake's Explanation

Drake later said that he had seen some strange ships moving west. He extinguished the light and went to investigate, taking with him the *Roebuck* and two pinnaces. The ships turned out to be German freighters, but on the way back to the fleet Drake came upon the stricken *Rosario*. It was in no shape to fight and quickly surrendered.

Drake was more fortunate than he knew. The *Rosario*, in addition to being a large warship, was carrying about one third of the Armada's money, meant to pay the duke of Parma's troops. He gladly transferred the treasure to his own ship and sped off to rejoin the fleet.

Later, Drake faced insinuations that he had deliberately left the fleet with the express purpose of capturing the *Rosario*. Frobisher was especially incensed, saying, as quoted in *Sir Francis Drake* by E.F. Benson, that if Drake refused to share his loot, he would take "the best blood in [Drake's] body."

The second encounter took place just off a spur of land known as Portland Bill on the day after Drake rejoined the fleet. The wind had shifted to the east, giving the Spaniards the weather gauge. Howard first tried to regain it by sailing around the Armada to the north and then to the south, but he was cut off both times.

Meanwhile, Frobisher had not followed Howard, but tried to squeeze between the Armada and Portland Bill along with five other ships. He failed to do so and came under severe attack. Drake, however, had been standing out to sea with about 50 ships. He knew from experience that the wind this time of year tended to shift during the morning. When it did, he launched such a fierce attack against the Armada's southern flank that the ships attacking Frobisher had to break off and come to the aid of their comrades.

The Isle of Wight

The battle lasted until the middle of the afternoon with very little result. No Spanish ships had been sunk, and the Armada continued its way down the channel. The big question was whether it would attempt to land on the Isle of Wight, a large diamond-shaped island off the port cities of Southampton and Portsmouth, England. For all Howard and Drake knew, the Spaniards were going to land an army on the island and use it as a base for invasion.

Medina Sidonia was, indeed, considering a landing on the Isle of Wight, but for the purpose of replenishing his food and water. The western end of the Solent, the channel between the island and mainland, was too narrow for the Armada, so he would have to sail around and enter from the eastern end.

Just as he was in position to do so, however, the southern end of his fleet came under attack. It was Drake again who had been biding his time, waiting for the right moment. When the southern end of the Armada fled to the east and threatened to separate from the main body, Medina Sidonia had no choice but to come to the rescue. By this time, the entire English fleet was between the Armada and the mouth of the Solent, and Medina Sidonia had no choice but to continue up the channel.

The European mainland was now only two days' sailing away. Since there was no deepwater port in the Netherlands, the Armada would have to rendezvous with Parma's barges at sea. Medina Sidonia had sent several messages to Parma in the Netherlands, asking when he would be ready. Having received no reply, he anchored the Armada off the northern French city of Calais.

Fireships

On the night of August 7, Howard, Drake, Frobisher, and Hawkins held a war council. They could not simply wait for Parma to link up with Medina Sidonia but had to find some way to dislodge the Armada. Their solution was fireships.

Fire was feared above all things by sailors in wooden ships. For centuries a tactic in naval warfare had been to fill a vessel with combustible materials, set it on fire, then let the wind carry it into the middle of an anchored enemy fleet. So it was that shortly after midnight, Spanish lookouts saw coming toward them a bright light that, as it grew nearer, revealed eight burning ships.

Medina Sidonia gave a signal for the Armada to haul in anchors and stand out to sea, but many captains panicked,

King Philip of Spain thought the Spanish Armada was too strong for England's Royal Navy, but events proved him wrong. Neither side was able to gain a clear advantage as the Armada sailed toward a rendezvous with a Spanish army in the Netherlands. Finally, the English employed fireships, unmanned ships packed with gunpowder and set ablaze. Although the fireships did not do any actual damage, they frightened the Spanish captains so much that their ships scattered.

cutting their anchor cables and scattering in all directions. The fireships had done no actual damage, but they had managed to accomplish what the English had failed do in three sea battles— break the Armada's formation.

When daylight revealed the Armada's plight off the town of Gravelines (then part of the Spanish Netherlands and the closest Spanish territory to England), Howard ordered an immediate attack. This time, with the Spanish ships scattered, the English ships ventured closer, and their bombardment did more damage. Drake was in the thick of the fighting. His *Revenge* was hit more than 40 times, and twice Drake's cabin was pierced by cannonballs.

The battle broke off at nightfall but continued the next day. The primary danger to the Armada, however, was not the English but a strong west wind that threatened to drive the ships onto the sandbanks at Dunkirk. As the water grew more shallow, some of Medina Sidonia's officers urged him to take the banner that had been blessed by the pope and escape in a small boat. The duke refused, and just as it appeared the fleet would be lost, the wind shifted and the Spaniards were able to escape, sailing into the North Sea.

The Armada Retreats

The English followed, but the great Armada had undergone such damage that Medina Sidonia was convinced it could not fight its way back south to link up with the duke of Parma. Its only choice was to continue north, sailing completely around the British Isles and back to Spain. Shipwrecks and murderous natives along the Irish coast took a fearful toll, and of the 130 ships that had left Corunna, only about 60 made it back home. Between 15,000 and 20,000 men had died.

Drake was not among those following the Armada. He had departed from the battle of Gravelines on the first day after writing to Walsingham, as quoted by Sugden, that "God hath given us so good a day . . . as I hope in God the Prince of Parma and Duke of Sidonia shall not shake hands these few days."

Drake had been detached by Howard to carry some high-ranking prisoners to London. This infuriated Frobisher, who claimed that Drake had once more deserted the fleet in search of loot. Later he charged, as quoted by Sugden, that Drake "gave them . . . his broadside . . . and was glad that he was gone again, like a cowardly knave or traitor—I rest doubtful, but the one I will swear."

The Armada had been defeated, and the threat of invasion had passed—for the moment. Spain had been wounded, but not fatally. Queen Elizabeth and her counselors were afraid that King Philip might mount another attempt. They decided to strike while their enemy was weakened, and the person they turned to for command was Francis Drake.

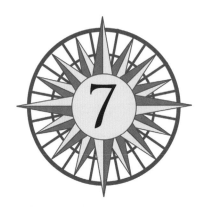

Last Voyages

THE DEFEAT OF THE SPANISH ARMADA WOULD PROVE TO BE the pinnacle of Francis Drake's career. His final two voyages were abject failures. His reputation, however, would outlive these disappointments, and he has gone down in history as one of Great Britain's greatest heroes.

The English did not realize how complete their victory had been. They had seen the Armada limp off into the North Sea, but they did not know how quickly another attempt might be made. Everyone, including Queen Elizabeth, thought there should be some sort of preventive counterstrike, but there was disagreement as to where and how.

There was little doubt, however, as to who should lead such an attack. Drake's status and popularity, already high after his voyage around the world and the raid on Cadiz, had reached a new level after the Armada victory.

Drake, with his usual eye toward plunder, thought the time would be perfect to capture the Azores (located about

Drake, victorious and famous, seemed to represent the glories of Elizabethan England. He built his reputation on his success as a privateer, a politician, and an explorer, and reached another level of status with his victory against the Spanish Armada. The queen and her privateers became overconfident, however, and disastrous military campaigns against Spanish America followed.

950 miles, or 1,500 kilometers, from Lisbon) and use it as a base for raids on Spanish shipping. Queen Elizabeth and Burghley had the destruction of the Spanish fleet as their top priority. Then there was Dom Antonio, former ruler of Portugal, who wanted England to restore his throne. Such a move would be a severe blow to Spain and also provide England with a valuable ally. Individually, any of these plans had a good chance for

success. The problem was that they were combined into one large, overambitious mission.

It would be a very expensive mission, as well. The Armada and the war in the Netherlands had depleted Elizabeth's treasury, but she did agree to contribute £20,000 and six ships. The rest would have to be raised from private investors. Sir John Norris, who was to command the land forces, offered £2,000, Drake and some associates gave £8,000, a merchant group put in another £5,000, and the City of London added £10,000.

Many Delays

The mission's best chance of success was to strike quickly, but such was not the case. Seasoned soldiers proved hard to find since so many were needed in the Netherlands. Queen Elizabeth, as usual, delayed for months before making a final commitment. Some investors backed out, and the lack of money made it difficult to get enough provisions. Drake fell ill and was unable to direct operations, and the voyage—first conceived in the weeks after the Armada in August—did not sail until the following April, in 1589.

The expedition was the largest combined naval and military force in English history—about 180 ships carrying 13,000 soldiers and 4,000 sailors. Drake wanted to head straight for Lisbon but had to heed the queen's top priority—destruction of the Armada's surviving ships. Instead of sailing to the Spanish port city of Santander, where about 40 such ships were known to be, he went to Corunna, claiming later that the wind was not right for a course to Santander and that he had heard rumors of Spanish ships at Corunna.

If Drake had, indeed, heard such rumors, they were false. Only seven large ships and a scattering of small boats awaited the invaders. These were pillaged and burned, and Norris's soldiers sacked the town, killing more than 500 citizens and soldiers. The English also seized great quantities of food supplies and about 150 pieces of artillery. It was far less than Drake had hoped for.

When it was time for the fleet to leave Corunna, it was pinned down for two weeks by adverse winds. The delay saw much of the supplies consumed and disease began to take its toll. By the time Drake and Norris sailed on May 8, they felt they had to decide between Santander or Lisbon. Drake followed his own desires instead of the queen's and headed for Lisbon.

Landing at Peniche

For some unknown reason Drake and Norris chose to land 6,000 soldiers at Peniche, about 50 miles (80 km) north of Lisbon, instead of at Cascais at the mouth of the Tagus River less than 20 miles (32 km) from the city. The plan was for Norris and the troops, accompanied by Dom Antonio, to march to Lisbon in anticipation that the Portuguese would flock to the side of whom they thought to be the rightful king. Drake would sail to Cascais and then up the Tagus to Lisbon to coordinate with Norris's arrival.

King Philip's commander in Lisbon was fully prepared, having been warned months before by spies that an attempt might be made to enthrone Dom Antonio. To make sure there would be no popular uprising, he had the leading opponents of Spanish rule arrested and either executed or jailed.

Thus when the English forces reached the outskirts of Lisbon on May 23 after a grueling five-day march, they found only a few brave individuals instead of an army welcoming them. One report, quoted by Sugden, said that Dom Antonio was greeted only by "a company of poor peasants . . . and one gentlewoman who presented the king with a basket of cherries and plums."

Norris and Dom Antonio waited in vain for the expected uprising. They also waited for Drake, who was still at Cascais. It is not known whether he was unaware of Norris's movements and late in sailing to Lisbon or whether he hesitated for some other reason. At any rate, this was hardly the Drake of old, dashing boldly into Cadiz.

By the time Drake finally decided on May 25 to move toward Lisbon, Norris had already begun retreating down the Tagus toward Cascais. By the time he made connection with the fleet, one-third of his force had been killed.

Waiting for Relief

The fleet and army waited at Cascais, hoping for reinforcements from England. Instead, they received word that the queen was furious that Santander had not been attacked and would send no more troops or weapons. The only good news was the arrival a few days later of 15 ships loaded with much-needed grain.

The arrival of fresh supplies led Drake to try to salvage the expedition by capturing the Azores and thus cutting the supply line between Spain and the Americas. The fleet sailed north and captured the Spanish town of Vigo. Here, Drake took 20 ships, leaving Norris to return to England with the rest.

Drake set out for the Azores on June 22 and promptly ran into a huge storm. By the time the fleet was reassembled and the damage assessed, he decided to give up the plan and return to England.

A chilly welcome awaited him there. At the end of May, Queen Elizabeth had written Drake and Norris, reminding them that they had assured her, as quoted by Kelsey, that their "first and principal action should be to take and distress the King of Spain's navy" and, if they had not, they must "be content to be reputed as traitors." When she learned the full extent of the failure, she ordered her council to summon the two commanders to London to face charges.

The inquiry was eventually dropped, but the reputation of the "golden knight" was sadly tarnished. People were saying, according to a report quoted by Kelsey, that, although the English had fought bravely, "their leaders were craven and the expedition came to nought." Another account, never substantiated, said that when Drake returned to Plymouth he was mobbed by women whose husbands had died or been killed.

Nichols's Book

He would try to rehabilitate his reputation by collaborating with Philip Nichols, his former shipmate and secretary, on a book about his 1572–1573 raid on Panama. He opened by dedicating the book to the queen, saying he wished to counter reports "whereby many untruths have been published, and the certain truth concealed." Her Majesty must have been unmoved, because permission to publish the book was refused. Only in 1626 did it appear as *Sir Francis Drake Revived.*

So out of favor was Drake that he would not see service at sea again for six years, but he was far from idle during that time. In April of 1590 there were rumors of another Spanish attack by sea. Elizabeth's council wrote to Drake, who was living at Buckland, asking him to take part in improving Plymouth's defenses. In addition to some improvements on the castle guarding the harbor, Drake recommended a new fort be built and contributed a large sum of money toward the project, which was eventually completed after his death.

England did, indeed, seem to be on the verge of another war with Spain. Drake was not at sea, but many of his associates were, capturing almost any foreign ship they came across, whether from enemy or ally. When merchants in friendly countries complained, Drake was appointed a commissioner for the causes of reprisal. This commission was to inventory prize ships and plunder brought into port and judge whether they should be returned to their owners.

In Parliament Again

Drake also became active again in parliament, being named a member for Plymouth in 1593. He served on several committees, including one to set up a pension for wounded soldiers and sailors and another to halt the manufacture of inferior cordage, or ropes, for ships. The main business before parliament, however, was a request to grant three subsidies, or payments, to the queen to build up the military. Drake,

DRAKE'S DRUM

One of the artifacts on display at Drake's former home, Buckland Abbey, is a drum 21 inches high with a barrel made of walnut. Although there is no proof, it is said to have been Francis Drake's and to have accompanied him on his voyage around the world in 1577–1580.

Legends grew up around the drum. A former Buckland Abbey housekeeper, as quoted in John Sugden's *Sir Francis Drake*, said that if Drake were to hear the drum beating, he would "rise and have a revel."

Sir Henry Newbolt turned the legends into a poem "Drake's Drum," written in 1895. In his version, however, the beating of the drum in times of national emergency would cause Drake to rise from the dead to come to his country's aid. According to the poem, Drake said as he lay dying,

> *Take my drum to England, hang et by the shore,*
> *Strike et when your powder's runnin' low;*
> *If the Dons [Spaniards] sign Devon,*
> *I'll quit the port o' Heaven,*
> *An' drum them up the Channel*
> *as we drummed them long ago.*

During World War I, a British colonel, E.T. Clifford, wrote that "the spirit of Drake is still with us, and still animates the people of this Empire. That is the true significance of Drake's Drum. Confidence, resolution, bravery and patriotism were Drake's characteristics. Let us follow so great an example."

having suffered from a lack of supplies on his recently failed voyage, spoke forcefully in favor. It was the only speech he is known to have made in Parliament, which recorded him, as quoted by Sugden, as describing "the King of Spain's strength and cruelty."

If there was to be a war, however, Drake wanted to be part of it. As early as 1592 he was trying to convince John Hawkins that a major raid on the West Indies should be mounted. The queen, always on the lookout for treasure, agreed, but it would not be until 1595 that the voyage would actually take place with Drake and Hawkins sharing command.

Neither Drake nor Hawkins likely relished such an arrangement. Drake's "forsaking" at San Juan d'Ulau stood between them, and they were opposites in temperament. One of their captains, Thomas Maynarde, wrote, as quoted by Sugden, that they were "men of so different natures and dispositions that what the one desireth the other would commonly oppose against . . . whom the one loved the other smally esteemed."

Philip Makes Ready

The fleet—54 ships in two squadrons—was supposed to sail on May 1, 1595, but was delayed until the last week of August. By this time, spies had informed King Philip that Drake and Hawkins were heading for the Caribbean, and he took steps to increase defenses there.

Drake and Hawkins clashed from the start over a shortage of supplies. Hawkins refused to take on some of Drake's men, accusing Drake of having skimped on food and water. When Drake wanted to stop in the Canary Islands for water, Hawkins agreed only after Drake threatened to go alone.

The fleet had no sooner reached its first objective—Puerto Rico—on November 12 than Hawkins died. He had been ill during the voyage, and Drake had agreed, against his better judgment, to a delay in the Antilles.

The delay meant that the Puerto Rican capital, San Juan, was on guard. New guns had been mounted on the harbor fortress and more on shore. Two ships had been sunk at the mouth of the harbor to block any attempt at entry.

The fleet anchored in El Cabrón Bay but soon had to retreat before Spanish fire. Drake was nearly killed when a cannonball smashed through his cabin, knocked his chair from under him, and wounded four companions, one fatally.

The next night the English sent a number of small boats around the blockage into the harbor where they succeeded in setting some Spanish frigates on fire, but that was the extent of the damage. Drake decided that San Juan was too well fortified, and the fleet departed a few days later having nothing to show for its efforts.

Panama was the primary target of the expedition, and Drake should have headed there at once before word of his presence spread. Instead, he spent more than a month raiding the northern coast of South America near Cartagena, burning four towns to the ground, including Rio de la Hacha.

Back at Panama

Drake finally reached the Panamanian coast on December 17, landing at Nombre de Dios, scene of his triumph more than two decades before. This time it was much different. A small group of Spanish soldiers put up a brief defense and then fled into the hills, but when Drake and his men took the town, they found only empty streets and houses. The people, amply warned, had evacuated, taking almost everything of value with them.

Drake now had to decide which route his land forces would take to the city of Panama on the Pacific coast. The most logical, because it was the rainy season, was up the Chagres River in small boats. Drake, thinking the river route would be defended, chose instead to send Thomas Baskerville on the overland road.

Baskerville and his troops left on December 29 and for two days made their way up and down hills, slogging through mud most of the time. The English had gone about 30 miles (48 km)—about halfway—when they were confronted by a small fortress squarely across their path. They tried to break through but were driven back repeatedly, losing upwards of 70 men. At last, Baskerville gave up and retreated back to Nombre de Dios.

Drake tried to rally the spirits of his men. There were other rich targets, he told them, but it was evident that he was deeply depressed. Maynarde wrote, as quoted by Bradford, "Since our return from Panama, he never carried mirth nor joy in his face."

The fleet sailed north to the island of Escudo to rest and replenish supplies, but a deadly fever soon took hold. Many men died and many more were sickened—including Drake. For the first time in his long seagoing career he remained in his cabin unable to come on deck.

His Final Days

He was still bedridden on January 23 when the fleet left Escudo and sailed back southward. Four days later Drake was so ill that he knew he was dying. He dictated an addition to his will, declaring himself, as quoted by Sugden, to be "perfect of mind and memory . . . although sick in body."

Shortly after midnight, Drake became delirious. He fought his way out of bed and demanded, according to an account quoted by Whitfield, to be dressed in his armor so he "could die like a soldier." He raved on for a time but was finally persuaded to return to his bed. It was there, at about 4 A.M. on January 28, 1596, that Francis Drake died.

The next day the ships anchored off the Panamanian town of Porto Bello, whose inhabitants fled on their arrival. Drake's body was sealed in a lead coffin aboard his flagship, the

Defiance. After a short sermon, and to the accompaniment of the thundering of guns fired in salute, the coffin was lowered into the sea. As a final and fitting tribute to their often violent leader, Drake's men left Porto Bello in flames.

Drake's Legacy

Drake's role as an explorer has been overshadowed by his fame as a privateer, the terror of the West Indies, and a hero of the defeat of the Armada. And yet, although plunder rather than knowledge was always his utmost goal, he took great pride in going where no one had gone before, as evidenced when he stretched himself out on what he surmised to be the southern tip of South America.

He was the first, perhaps, to discover that there was open sea between South America and whatever lay to the south. Had he been more of an explorer and less of a pirate, he might have tried to confirm his discovery. But that knowledge lay to the east, and Spanish treasure to the west.

His exploration continued up the western coast of North America. He was perhaps the first European to land on the upper California coast, the first to see what later would become Canada, and the first to try to find a passage east across the top of North America.

Drake's fame as an explorer was lessened because details of his exploits were kept secret by the government. If there was, indeed, an alternate to the Strait of Magellan, England did not want Spain to know about it. It was only more than 20 years after his death that *The World Encompassed* told the story.

By that time, another image of Francis Drake had been firmly established—and, indeed, had been established during his lifetime—the image of the daring buccaneer, thumbing his

Drake's seafaring career continued and he suffered several defeats in a row. In 1596, he died of dysentery while anchored off the coast of Panama. He was buried in a lead coffin at sea off Porto Bello.

nose at the king of Spain, going anywhere, taking anything, and eluding all attempts to capture him. It was this image of Drake that entered the national consciousness. His amazing self-confidence and bravado when the odds were against him transferred themselves to future generations of British sailors. The spirit of Drake against the Armada, it might be said,

IN HIS ENEMIES' EYES

Francis Drake aroused a mixture of fear and respect in the many enemies with whom he dealt over his career. A survivor of the Spanish Armada wrote that he "was a devil, and no man." And yet one of his prisoners, Don Francisco de Zárate, complimented his captor as "very polite."

Another Spaniard, Santo Domingo official Juan Melgarejo, wrote that Drake was "sharp, restless, well-spoken, inclined to liberality and to ambition, vainglorious, boastful, not very cruel." And his exploits were praised by Pope Sixtus V, who said, "Just look at Drake! Who is he? What forces has he? And yet he burned twenty-five of the King's ships at Gibraltar, and as many again at Lisbon. He has robbed the flotilla and sacked Santo Domingo. His reputation is so great that his countrymen flock to him to share his booty."

Drake cast a long shadow even after his death. In 1598 Spanish poet and playwright Lope de Vega wrote "La Dragontea." Even though the epic poem condemned and vilified Drake, it acknowledged his lingering effect on Spain. One excerpt, warns that

> He who alive to them a danger was,
> Shall be a danger unto them again;
> For with his death his terror shall not pass,
> But still amid the air he shall remain.

The quotation from "La Dragontea" is from John Cummins's article "'That Golden Knight': Drake and His Reputation." All others are from *Sir Francis Drake* by John Sugden.

would find echoes in that of Horatio Nelson against the forces of Napoleon at Trafalgar more than 200 years later. And it would be in this spirit that Great Britain would eventually, in the words of the song, "rule the waves."

The elements of boldness and adventure, of always seeking a new horizon, were marked in Drake much as in other explorers. He expressed it himself in a poem written in 1577 just before embarking on his epic journey around the world. As found on the Web site of the Fitzroy Presbyterian Church in Belfast, Northern Ireland, it reads, in part,

> Disturb us, Lord, to dare more boldly,
> To venture on wilder seas
> Where storms will show Your mastery;
> Where losing sight of land,
> We shall find the stars.
>
> We ask you to push back
> The horizons of our hopes;
> And to push back the future
> In strength, courage, hope, and love.

CHRONOLOGY

c.1540	Francis Drake born near Tavistock, England.
1566–1567	Serves on slave-trading voyage commanded by John Lovell.
1567–1569	Accompanies John Hawkins on slave-trading voyage; Spaniards defeat Hawkins at San Juan d'Ulau.
1569	Marries Mary Newman on July 4.

TIMELINE

1567–1569
Accompanies John Hawkins on slave-trading voyage; Spaniards defeat Hawkins at San Juan d'Ulau

1577–1580
Completes voyage around the world

1540

1572

c.1540 Francis Drake born near Tavistock, England

1567

1580

1572–1573
Third raid on the West Indies makes him rich

1570–1571	Commands his first two raids on the West Indies.
1572–1573	Drake's third raid on the West Indies makes him rich.
1577–1580	Undertakes and completes voyage around the world.
1581	JANUARY 16 Takes seat as member of Parliament.
	APRIL 4 Knighted by Queen Elizabeth aboard the *Golden Hind*.
	SEPTEMBER 17 Elected lord mayor of Plymouth.
1585	Marries Elizabeth Sydenham on February 9.
1585–1586	The "Great Raid" in the West Indies is a financial failure.
1587	Drake raids Spanish fleet in Cadiz harbor.

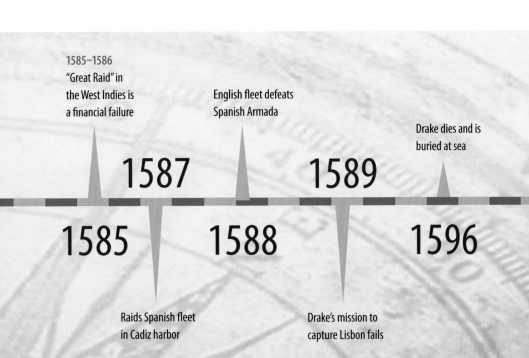

1585–1586
"Great Raid" in the West Indies is a financial failure

English fleet defeats Spanish Armada

Drake dies and is buried at sea

1587

1589

1585

1588

1596

Raids Spanish fleet in Cadiz harbor

Drake's mission to capture Lisbon fails

1588	English fleet defeats Spanish Armada.
1589	Drake's mission to capture Lisbon fails.
1595	Drake sails with John Hawkins on final mission.
1596	JANUARY 28 Dies and is buried at sea.

GLOSSARY

BARK   A small vessel that is propelled by oars or sails

BLOCKADE   To close off a place, such as a port or city, with hostile ships or troops

BOOTY   Valuables taken from an enemy in war; something seized by violence or robbery

BROADSIDE   The simultaneous discharge of all the guns on one side of a warship

CLOVE   The dried flower bud of a tropical tree used whole or ground as a spice

CORSAIR   A pirate

DYSENTERY   A disorder of the lower intestinal tract, usually caused by a bacterial or parasitic infection. Causes pain, fever, and severe diarrhea.

FRIGATE   A high-speed, medium-sized sailing war vessel

GALLEY   A seagoing vessel propelled mainly by oars

HOBNOB   To associate with on very friendly terms

HOLD   The entire cargo space within the hull of a ship

ISTHMUS   A narrow strip of land, bordered on both sides by water, connecting two larger bodies of land

MASTER   The ship's officer in charge of navigation

MERCHANTMAN   A ship used mostly to carry cargo for trading

PINNACE   A small ship that could be either sailed or rowed; usually used in attendance on a larger ship

PRIVATEER A sea captain who, though not a naval officer, receives a commission to raid enemy ports and/or shipping

RECONNAISSANCE A search made for useful information

SPAR A wooden or metal pole used to support sails and rigging

TAFFETA A crisp, smooth, lustrous fabric

VICEROY Person appointed to rule as a deputy of the monarch

WINCH To move something with a rope attached to a revolving drum

BIBLIOGRAPHY

Benson, E. F. *Sir Francis Drake*. New York: Harper and Brothers Publishers, 1927.

Bradford, Ernle. *The Wind Commands Me*. New York: Harcourt, Brace & World, 1965.

Cummins, John. "'That Golden Knight': Drake and His Reputation." *History Today*, January 1, 1996, 14–21.

Drake, Francis, et al., *The World Encompassed*, 1628. Contained in John Hampden, editor, *Francis Drake: Privateer*. Birmingham: University of Alabama Press, 1972.

Hampden, John, ed., *Francis Drake: Privateer*. Birmingham: University of Alabama Press, 1972.

Hawkins, John. *The Third Troublesome Voyage Made With the* Jesus of Lubeck, *the* Minion *and Four Other Ships to the Parts of Guinea and the West Indies, in the Years 1567 and 1568, 1569*. Contained in John Hampden, editor, *Francis Drake: Privateer*. Birmingham: University of Alabama Press, 1972.

Kelsey, Harry. *Sir Francis Drake: The Queen's Pirate*. New Haven, Conn.: Yale University Press, 1998.

Nichols, Philip. *Sir Francis Drake Revived*, 1626. Contained in John Hampden, editor, *Francis Drake: Privateer*. Birmingham: University of Alabama Press, 1972.

Sugden, John. *Sir Francis Drake*. New York: Henry Holt and Company, 1990.

Whitfield, Peter. *Sir Francis Drake*. New York: New York University Press, 2004.

FURTHER RESOURCES

Bawlf, Samuel. *The Secret Voyage of Sir Francis Drake: 1577–1580.* New York: Penguin, 2004.

Champion, Neil. *Sir Francis Drake.* Chicago, Ill.: Heinman Library, 2001.

Hynson, Colin. *Queen Elizabeth and the Spanish Armada.* Grand Rapids, Mich.: School Specialty Publishing, 2006.

Lace, William W. *Defeat of the Spanish Armada.* San Diego: Lucent Books, 1997.

———. *Elizabethan England.* San Diego: Lucent Books, 1995.

Marrin, Albert. *The Sea King: Sir Francis Drake and His Times.* New York: Atheneum Books for Young Readers, 1995.

Stewart, David. *You Wouldn't Want to Explore with Sir Francis Drake!: A Pirate You'd Rather Not Know.* New York: Children's Press, 2005.

WEB SITES

Explorers
http://edtech.kennesaw.edu/web/explorer.html
Informative page created at Kennesaw State University links to information about many famous explorers.

The Mariner's Museum: Francis Drake
http://www.mariner.org/educationalad/ageofex/drake.php
One of the largest international maritime history museums chronicles the developments in shipbuilding, ocean navigation, and cartography that made the voyages of the fifteenth through eighteenth centuries possible. Focuses on famous explorers such as Francis Drake, James Cook, etc.

Sir Francis Drake
http://www.mcn.org/2/oseeler/drake.htm
Links to Web sites—some scholarly, some just for fun—dealing with Drake's voyage around the world.

PICTURE CREDITS

INDEX

ABOUT
THE AUTHOR

WILLIAM W. LACE is a native of Fort Worth, Texas, where he is executive assistant to the chancellor at Tarrant County College. He holds a bachelor's degree from Texas Christian University, a master's degree from East Texas State University, and a doctorate from the University of North Texas. Prior to joining Tarrant County College, he was director of the News Service at the University of Texas at Arlington and a sportswriter and columnist for the *Fort Worth Star-Telegram*. He has written 50 nonfiction books for young readers on subjects ranging from the atomic bomb to the Dallas Cowboys. He and his wife, Laura, a retired school librarian, live in Arlington, Texas, and have two children and four grandchildren.